FEDERAL SPEECHES

POLICY AND PRACTICES

GOVERNMENT PROCEDURES AND OPERATIONS

Additional books in this series can be found on Nova's website under the Series tab.

Additional e-books in this series can be found on Nova's website under the e-book tab.

FEDERAL SPEECHES

POLICY AND PRACTICES

KATHLEEN WELDON
EDITOR

New York

Library of Congress Cataloging-in-Publication Data

ISBN: 978-1-61761-755-3

Published by Nova Science Publishers, Inc. † New York

CONTENTS

PREFACE

This book discusses the tradition, function, and policy implications of the State of the Union address. It also discusses special order speeches and other forms of non-legislative debate in the house; one-minute speeches; morning hour debates; and the constitutional background and recent developments of the speech or debate clause.

Chapter 1 - The State of the Union address is a communication between the President and Congress in which the chief executive reports on the current conditions of the United States and provides policy proposals for the upcoming legislative year. Formerly known as the "Annual Message," the State of the Union address originates in the Constitution. As part of the system of checks and balances, Article II, Section 3, clause 1 mandates that the President "shall from time to time give to the Congress Information of the State of the Union, and recommend to their Consideration such Measures as he shall judge necessary and expedient." In recent decades, the President has expanded his State of the Union audience, addressing the speech to both the nation and Members of Congress.

Over time, the State of the Union address has evolved considerably. The format and delivery of the speech have changed, and its length has fluctuated widely. Technology has also influenced the delivery of the address, with the advent of radio, television, and the Internet playing significant roles in the transformation.

Although each President uses the State of the Union address to outline his administration's policy agenda, most incorporate common rhetorical arguments and ceremonial traditions. Bipartisanship, attention to both the past and the future, and optimism are recurring themes in State of the Union addresses.

The legislative success rate of policy proposals mentioned in State of the Union addresses varies widely. Addresses given after a President's election or reelection and during periods of unified party government tend to produce higher rates of legislative success. Presidents can also use the State of the Union address to increase media attention for a particular issue.

Immediately following the State of the Union address, the political party not occupying the White House provides an opposition response. The response, usually much shorter than the State of the Union, outlines the opposition party's policy agenda and serves as an official rejoinder to the proposals outlined by the President.

Chapter 2 - Rules in the House of Representatives typically limit the time allowed for floor speeches and require debate to be germane to pending business. A series of unanimous consent practices have evolved that permit Members to address the House for specified durations and at specified times on subjects of their own choosing, outside the consideration of legislative business. The principal forms of such *non-legislative debate* are *special order speeches*, *one-minute speeches*, and *morning hour debates*.

Chapter 3 - Special order speeches (commonly called "special orders") usually take place at the end of the day after the House has completed all legislative business. During the special order period, individual Representatives deliver speeches on topics of their choice for up to 60 minutes.

Special orders provide one of the few opportunities for non-legislative debate in the House. They also give Members a chance to speak outside the time restrictions that govern legislative debate in the House and the Committee of the Whole.

The rules of the House do not provide for special order speeches. Instead, special orders have evolved as a *unanimous consent practice* of the House. Recognition for special orders is the prerogative of the Speaker. During the special order period, Members must abide by the rules of the House, the chamber's precedents, and the "Speaker's announced policies," in that order. The term "Speaker's announced policies" refers to the Speaker's policies on certain aspects of House procedure.

In practice, the Speaker's current policies on special orders (announced on January 6, 2009) govern recognition for special order speeches as well as the reservation and television broadcast of these speeches. Under these announced policies, there are generally three "stages" to each day's special order period:

- first, five-minute special orders by *individual Members*;
- next, special orders longer than five minutes (normally 60 minutes in length) by *the party's leadership or a designee*; and
- last, special orders longer than five minutes (length varies from 6 to 60 minutes) by *individual Members*.

Members usually reserve special orders in advance through their party's leadership. Instead of delivering a special order speech on the House floor, Members may choose to insert their speech in either the House pages of the *Congressional Record* or the section known as the "Extensions of Remarks."

Reform proposals were advanced in recent Congresses to address both concerns about breaches in decorum during special order speeches and the costs of conducting these speeches.

Chapter 4 - Recognition for one-minute speeches (commonly called "one minutes") in the House of Representatives is the prerogative of the Speaker. A period for one minutes usually takes place at the beginning of the legislative day after the daily prayer, the Pledge of Allegiance, and approval of the previous day's *Journal*. During this time, Representatives ask unanimous consent to address the House for one minute on a topic of their choice. In addition, one-minute speeches are often permitted after legislative business ends, but before special order speeches begin.

The rules of the House do not provide for one-minute speeches. Instead, one minutes have evolved as a *unanimous consent practice* of the chamber. During one-minute speeches, Members must abide by the rules of the House, the chamber's precedents, and the "Speaker's announced policies," in that order. The term "Speaker's announced policies" refers to the Speaker's policies on certain aspects of House procedure, such as recognition for one minutes.

Representatives seeking recognition for one minutes sit in the first row on their party's side of the chamber. From the chair's vantage point, Republican Members sit on the left side of the chamber and Democratic Members on the right side. The chair moves from his right to left in recognizing Members on each side of the aisle. When recognized by the chair, individual Members ask unanimous consent to address the House for one minute and to revise and extend their remarks. Permission is almost always granted. Members deliver one-minute speeches from the well of the chamber. They are limited to one minute and cannot ask unanimous consent for additional time. Instead of delivering a one-minute speech on the House floor, a Member may ask unanimous consent to insert the speech in the House section of the *Congressional Record.*

Members need not reserve one-minute speeches in advance through their party's leadership. Nevertheless, the party leadership communication arms—known as the "Democratic Message Group" and the "Republican Theme Team" — sometimes coordinate party Members to deliver one minutes on the issue designated as the party's daily message. These party Members usually receive priority seating for recognition purposes.

Chapter 5 - On Mondays and Tuesdays, the House of Representatives meets earlier than the hour established for that day's session for a period called "morning hour debates" (also known as "morning hour speeches"). This period provides a rare opportunity for non-legislative debate in the House; remarks in the House are usually limited to pending legislative business. During morning hour debates, individual Members deliver speeches on topics of their choice for up to five minutes. The majority and minority leaders give the Speaker a list showing how each party's time for morning hour debates will be allocated among its Members. The chair follows this list in recognizing Members for morning hour debates. At the conclusion of morning hour debates, the House recesses until the starting time for that day's session. This report examines current House practices for morning hour debates and how these debates are used.

Chapter 6 - Members of Congress have immunity for their legislative acts under Article I, Section 6, clause 1, of the Constitution, which provides in part that "for any speech or debate in either House, [Senators and Representatives] shall not be questioned in any other place." Even if their actions are within the scope of the Speech or Debate Clause or some other legal immunity, Members of Congress remain accountable to the house of Congress in which they serve and to the electorate. In cases in which the Clause applies, the immunity is absolute and cannot be defeated by an allegation of an improper purpose or motivation. When applicable, the Clause provides both immunity from liability (in civil and criminal proceedings) and a complimentary evidentiary privilege.

Recently, two separate and previously unresolved issues arose with respect to the scope and application of the Speech or Debate Clause. The first case concerned claims of employment discrimination brought against Members' offices pursuant to the Congressional Accountability Act of 1995. Both the Tenth Circuit Court of Appeals and the D.C. Circuit ruled that the Speech or Debate Clause does not automatically prevent such suits from proceeding. Additionally, an appeal to the Supreme Court was rejected because the Court ruled that it lacked a jurisdictional basis to decide the case.

These decisions, however, appear to leave unanswered significant questions about the use and introduction of evidence related to "legislative acts," which are protected by the Speech or Debate Clause. Such questions could ultimately frustrate the ability of potential plaintiffs to pursue their claims successfully.

In August 2007, the Court of Appeals for the District of Columbia Circuit (D.C. Circuit) issued its opinion in a case arising from the execution of a search warrant on the Rayburn House Office of Representative William J. Jefferson. The search was conducted as part of the FBI's investigation of Representative Jefferson to determine whether he was involved in criminal activity, including bribery and other felonies. Such an action by the executive branch appears to be unprecedented. It raised significant constitutional questions about potential intimidation of the legislative branch and threats to its independence, which the Clause is designed to protect.

Although Representative Jefferson lost his initial legal challenge, the appeals court subsequently held that the search violated the Speech or Debate Clause. The court ordered the district court to provide Representative Jefferson with copies of the seized materials and a chance to assert his privilege claims ex parte and in camera. Moreover, the appeals court ordered that the Department of Justice (DOJ) continue to refrain from reviewing any of the seized materials until the privilege claims were evaluated by the lower court.

In 2011, the Ninth Circuit Court of Appeals also weighed in on how to apply the Clause to executive branch criminal investigations of Members. In that case, Representative Richard Renzi was accused of agreeing to support legislation in exchange for a private land purchase agreement benefitting one of his creditors. He was indicted on numerous criminal counts, including extortion and fraud, which he challenged on Speech or Debate Clause grounds.

The appeals court determined that his challenged actions were not covered by the Clause. Additionally, the Ninth Circuit appeared to split with the D.C. Circuit analysis in Representative Jefferson's case on whether the Clause prevents the executive branch from ever viewing protected evidence.

This report examines the constitutional background of the Speech or Debate Clause and these recent developments in jurisprudence.

In: Federal Speeches: Policy and Practices   ISBN: 978-1-61761-755-3
Editor: Kathleen Weldon   © 2014 Nova Science Publishers, Inc.

Chapter 1

THE PRESIDENT'S STATE OF THE UNION ADDRESS: TRADITION, FUNCTION, AND POLICY IMPLICATIONS[*]

Colleen J. Shogan and Thomas H. Neale

SUMMARY

The State of the Union address is a communication between the President and Congress in which the chief executive reports on the current conditions of the United States and provides policy proposals for the upcoming legislative year. Formerly known as the "Annual Message," the State of the Union address originates in the Constitution. As part of the system of checks and balances, Article II, Section 3, clause 1 mandates that the President "shall from time to time give to the Congress Information of the State of the Union, and recommend to their Consideration such Measures as he shall judge necessary and expedient." In recent decades, the President has expanded his State of the Union audience, addressing the speech to both the nation and Members of Congress.

Over time, the State of the Union address has evolved considerably. The format and delivery of the speech have changed, and its length has fluctuated widely. Technology has also influenced the delivery of the

---

[*] This is an edited, reformatted and augmented version of Congressional Research Service Publication, No. R40132, dated January 24, 2014.

address, with the advent of radio, television, and the Internet playing significant roles in the transformation.

Although each President uses the State of the Union address to outline his administration's policy agenda, most incorporate common rhetorical arguments and ceremonial traditions. Bipartisanship, attention to both the past and the future, and optimism are recurring themes in State of the Union addresses.

The legislative success rate of policy proposals mentioned in State of the Union addresses varies widely. Addresses given after a President's election or reelection and during periods of unified party government tend to produce higher rates of legislative success. Presidents can also use the State of the Union address to increase media attention for a particular issue.

Immediately following the State of the Union address, the political party not occupying the White House provides an opposition response. The response, usually much shorter than the State of the Union, outlines the opposition party's policy agenda and serves as an official rejoinder to the proposals outlined by the President.

OVERVIEW

The State of the Union address is a communication between the President and Congress in which the chief executive reports on the current conditions of the United States and provides policy proposals for the upcoming legislative year. Formerly known as the "Annual Message," the State of the Union address originates in the Constitution. As part of the system of checks and balances, Article II, Section 3, clause 1 requires that the President "shall from time to time give to the Congress Information of the State of the Union, and recommend to their Consideration such Measures as he shall judge necessary and expedient." In recent decades, the President has expanded his State of the Union audience, addressing the speech to both the nation and Members of Congress.

From the perspective of Congress, the State of the Union address may be considered the most important presidential speech of the year. Although Presidents may ask to address Congress in joint session on extraordinary occasions, the State of the Union is the one time Presidents are regularly scheduled to venture to the House chamber to present their programmatic priorities and set the tone for the ensuing year. Although modern Presidents communicate with Congress and the public consistently and persistently, the

State of the Union provides the President with a unique opportunity to present his entire policy platform in one speech.

From the President's perspective, the State of the Union address has evolved from a constitutional duty to a welcome source of executive power and authority. Standing before the American public to deliver the annual address, the President combines several constitutional roles: chief of state, chief executive, chief diplomat, commander-in-chief, and chief legislator.[1] Besides delivering the State of the Union, there is no other annual opportunity for the President to showcase his entire arsenal of constitutional powers.

Over time, the State of the Union address has evolved considerably. The format and delivery of the speech has changed, and its length has fluctuated widely. Technology has also influenced the delivery of the address, with the advent of radio, television, and the Internet playing significant roles in the transformation.

HISTORICAL PERSPECTIVE

As a rhetorical tool, the State of the Union Address has changed in several substantial ways since the origins of the American republic. It is difficult to point to one moment in time when the address developed into the contemporary speech now commonly recognized as the starting point of the legislative session.[2] Instead, several presidents throughout American history presided over shifts and variations to the address.

George Washington gave the first State of the Union Address on January 8, 1790. Washington's address, which was quite short at 1,089 words, was delivered before both houses of Congress.[3]

After Washington gave his second State of the Union address the following year, he established the precedent that the President would provide information annually to Congress.[4]

John Adams followed Washington's precedent during his tenure. Likening it to a "speech from the throne" reminiscent of monarchy's vestiges, Thomas Jefferson changed course and instead submitted his Annual Message in writing.[5] Historians also speculate that Jefferson was a poor public speaker and did not want to deliver the Annual Address orally since his Inaugural Address had been barely audible and was unfavorably received.[6] Between 1801 and 1913, Presidents fulfilled their constitutional duty by sending their yearly report as a formal written letter to Congress. These written messages contained information about the state of the nation, and also included policy recommendations. During this time period, the Annual Message swelled in length, with several exceeding 25,000 words.[7]

President Woodrow Wilson altered historical precedent when he delivered the 1913 Annual Message in the House chamber before a joint session of Congress. Although Wilson's action "stunned official Washington," he had written extensively in *Constitutional Government* about his disagreement with Jefferson's decision to submit the address in writing. Instead, Wilson read the Constitution as providing the President with the broad authority to serve as a national spokesman.[8] Wilson altered presidential rhetoric, using it as an intermediary tool to draw widespread public attention to the policies he supported. The public's endorsement served as political leverage that could compel Members of Congress to support his legislative agenda.

From 1913 until 1934, the Annual Message entered a transitional phase in which Presidents occasionally issued the address orally. Wilson delivered six of his eight Annual Messages in person, and Warren Harding presented two of his four addresses orally. Calvin Coolidge gave one address in the House chamber, and became the first President to broadcast the annual speech on radio.

During his presidential terms, Franklin Roosevelt solidified the oral tradition of the Annual Message. Roosevelt also applied the constitutional language "State of the Union," both to the message and the event, which became the popular nomenclature from his presidency forward. Given its oral rather than written delivery, the length of the address decreased to between 5,000 and 7,000 words. Roosevelt also ushered in the modern tradition of using the collective words "we" and "our" with greater frequency than his predecessors.

Figure 1 displays the length of State of the Union addresses across American presidential history.[9] The graph shows the sudden drop in 1913, when Woodrow Wilson resuscitated the oral mode of delivery. The spikes in **Figure 1** after Wilson are instances in which Presidents issued the final State of the Union of their term in writing, such as Franklin Roosevelt in 1945 and Carter in 1981. After winning reelection in 1972, Richard Nixon issued a series of written messages in 1973 instead of giving an overview speech. Barack Obama's 2013 speech contained 6,775 words, which was slightly shorter than his 2012 speech of 7,059 words.[10]

Harry Truman's 1947 State of the Union address was the first televised. Until 1965, Presidents issued the State of the Union during the day. To attract a larger viewing audience, Lyndon Johnson changed the time of the speech to the evening. This practice has been followed since Johnson, and Presidents now explicitly direct the address to the citizens of the United States as well as Congress.[11]

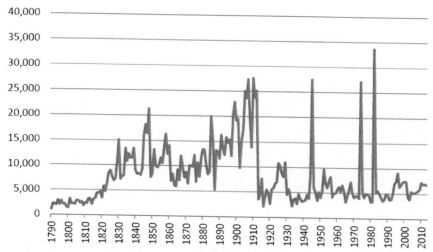

Source: Data provided by John Woolley and Gerhard Peters, *The American Presidency Project*, http://www.presidency accessed December 29, 2011.

Figure 1. Length of the State of the Union Addresses Number of Words, 1790-2013.

TRADITION AND CEREMONY

The State of the Union address is a speech steeped in tradition and ceremony. It is known for its display of pomp and circumstance, perhaps corroborating Thomas Jefferson's objection that the custom retains monarchical elements. In presenting the address, the President acts as both the head of government and the head of state. The combination of both roles makes the annual speech a uniquely powerful ritual.

Timing

Until the 20th amendment changed the timing for the new terms of Senators and Representatives to January 3, the annual message was routinely delivered in December. Since 1934, the President's annual message has been delivered on a range of dates, from January 3 to February 2. To attract television viewers across the United States, the address is normally presented at 9:00 in the evening, Eastern Standard Time.

Location, Seating, and Attendance

The State of the Union address is now customarily delivered in the House chamber of the Capitol, before a joint session of Congress. A concurrent resolution, agreed to by both chambers, sets aside an appointed time for a joint session of the House and Senate "for the purpose of receiving such communication as the President of the United States shall be pleased to make to them."[12]

Aside from reserved places for leadership, seats in the chamber are not assigned to Members. Any time during the day, House Members may claim a seat for the evening's address. They must, however, remain physically in the seat to retain their place for the speech.[13]

At the designated time, Senators cross the Capitol to the House chamber, where seats are reserved for them as a group at the front of the chamber. The Speaker and the Vice President (in his capacity as President of the Senate) occupy seats on the dais, and the Speaker presides. Seats in the well of the House chamber are reserved for the President's Cabinet, Justices of the Supreme Court who choose to attend, the Joint Chiefs of Staff, former Members of Congress, and members of the diplomatic corps.[14]

In accord with long-standing custom and to ensure the continuity of government, one Cabinet secretary does not attend the speech. After September 11, 2001, congressional leadership began designating two Members from each house of Congress, representing both parties, to remain absent from the Capitol during the President's speech.

At the January 25, 2011, State of the Union, Members of Congress broke from tradition and sat next to Members of the opposing party. In previous years, Members have taken their seats in a bifurcated fashion, choosing to sit with Members of their own party. In a "Dear Colleague" letter written two weeks before the speech, Senator Mark Udall urged Members of both chambers "to cross the aisle and sit together."[15] Members of Congress have continued the bipartisan practice of seating since 2011.

Special Guests

Seating in the gallery is restricted to ticket holders and is coordinated by the House Sergeant at Arms. Each Member of Congress receives one chamber ticket, with a specific reserved seat, for the address. Congressional leadership and the White House receive multiple tickets.[16]

Since 1982, in a new tradition established by Ronald Reagan, Presidents frequently ask guests to join the First Lady in the gallery. These individuals usually have performed an act of heroism or achieved an impressive milestone that illustrates an important theme in the President's speech. At the appropriate time, the President acknowledges the guests seated adjacent to the First Lady and identifies their particular contribution. Presidential speechwriters refer to these guests as "Lenny Skutniks" in reference to the first guest highlighted by Reagan in 1982.[17] Recent guests have included Representative Gabrielle Giffords, Tim Cook (CEO of Apple, Inc.), Sammy Sosa, Julie Aigner-Clark (CEO of Baby Einstein), Rosa Parks, Hamid Karzai, Dikembe Mutombo, former Treasury Secretary and Senator Lloyd Bentsen, Hank Aaron, Wesley Autrey (who rescued a man on the New York City subway tracks), and numerous active military service members and veterans.

COMMON ELEMENTS

The State of the Union address is a unique genre of presidential speech. Historian Charles Beard commented, "Whatever may be its purport, the message is the one great public document of the United States which is widely read and discussed."[18] Karlyn Kohrs Campbell and Kathleen Hall Jamieson have identified three repetitive, sequential rhetorical arguments in State of the Union addresses:

- public meditations on values;
- assessments of information and issues; and
- policy recommendations.[19]

The Sequence of Arguments

These three rhetorical arguments typically occur in a predictable sequential order. The President offers his opinion concerning important values or national character. Such an assessment leads him to identify targeted issues that will constitute his legislative agenda. Finally, he offers specific policy recommendations. The iteration of values, issue identification, and policy recommendations typically repeats itself numerous times in a State of the Union speech.

For example, in his 1962 address, President John F. Kennedy identified the values he deemed critically important to the nation:

> But a stronger nation and economy require more than a balanced Budget. They require progress in those programs that spur our growth and fortify our strength.

He then recognized the policy problem that arose from the values he emphasized:

> A strong America also depends on its farms and natural resources.... Our task is to master and turn to fully fruitful ends the magnificent productivity of our farms and farmers. The revolution on our own countryside stands in the sharpest contrast to the repeated farm failures of the Communist nations and is a source of pride to us all.

Finally, Kennedy provided his specific policy recommendation:

> I will, therefore, submit to the Congress a new comprehensive farm program—tailored to fit the use of our land and the supplies of each crop to the long-range needs of the sixties—and designed to prevent chaos in the sixties with a program of commonsense.[20]

Presidents use this three-part rhetorical sequence when discussing both domestic and foreign policy in the State of the Union.

Recurring Themes

In addition to a common sequence of rhetorical arguments, State of the Union addresses also exhibit recurring thematic elements. Most include rhetoric about the past and future, bipartisanship, and optimism.

Past and the Future

Typically, the speech focuses on both past accomplishments and future goals. State of the Union addresses pay homage to the historical achievements of the nation and its recurring national values. In his 1983 address, Ronald Reagan stated the following:

> The very key to our success has been our ability, foremost among nations, to preserve our lasting values by making change work for us rather than against us.[21]

Through attention to both past and future, Presidents can use the State of the Union address to develop their own definition of the national identity. For example, Bill Clinton used his 1995 speech to introduce the concept of a "New Covenant" that blended the traditional themes of "opportunity and responsibility" with the current policy challenges his Administration faced. Moving back and forth between historical themes and contemporary issues is a common rhetorical practice in State of the Union addresses. Using the past to explain legislative proposals and decisions is a method aimed at legitimizing the President's policy program.

Bipartisanship

The State of the Union address is not primarily a partisan speech or document. The bipartisan tone of the speech distinguishes it from other types of presidential rhetoric.[22] Speaking before a joint session of Congress, Presidents often try to frame their arguments in such a way to build consensus. In his 2002 speech, George W. Bush stated the following:

> September the 11th brought out the best in America and the best in this Congress. And I join the American people in applauding your unity and resolve. Now Americans deserve to have this same spirit directed toward addressing problems here at home. I'm a proud member of my party. Yet as we act to win the war, protect our people, and create jobs in America, we must act, first and foremost, not as Republicans, not as Democrats but as Americans.[23]

A rhetorical emphasis on bipartisanship can be politically empowering. By claiming a willingness to reach across the aisle, Presidents can remind listeners that their constitutional authority includes a mandate to protect the welfare of all citizens. Such a claim is unique to the presidency, and can serve as a powerful component of the chief executive's national leadership.

Optimism

The final recurring theme is optimism. No matter how terrible the crisis facing the country, Presidents always adopt a can-do "Horatio Alger" tone in their annual speech.[24] Only a month after the attack on Pearl Harbor, Franklin Roosevelt began his 1942 State of the Union address with the following statement:

> In fulfilling my duty to report on the State of the Union, I am proud to say to you that the spirit of the American people was never higher than it is today—the Union was never more closely knit together—this country was never more deeply determined to face the solemn tasks before it. The response of the American people has been instantaneous, and it will be sustained until our security is assured.[25]

Presidents often acknowledge the difficult nature of the goals they set, but such acknowledgement is qualified by a strong statement that Americans will always fulfill their destiny, solve intractable problems, and ultimately "establish a more perfect Union." No President has ever reported that the crisis facing the nation was insurmountable.[26]

POLICY IMPACT

The State of the Union address is uniquely situated to strengthen the President's role as chief legislator. The President routinely uses the address to convey his policy priorities and advertise his past legislative successes. In the course of the speech, Presidents can advocate for policies already being considered by Congress, introduce innovative ideas, or threaten vetoes.[27]

Prior to Woodrow Wilson's precedent-changing personal appearances before joint sessions, Presidents from Thomas Jefferson forward directed their annual address mainly to Congress, although major newspapers and magazines analyzed the contents of the speech. Now that the State of the Union is broadcast on television, radio, and the Internet, Presidents can speak directly to Congress and the American public. By speaking directly to citizens, Presidents attempt to convince the public to pressure their elected Representatives and Senators to support particular policy proposals mentioned in the speech. From 1965 through 2002, the median level of policy requests in a State of the Union address was 31.[28]

Progression of Presidential Term

Presidents often change the emphasis of their State of the Union addresses as their term in office progresses. Electoral pressures, the state of his relationship with Congress, and the President's past legislative record influence such a development.

First Year Addresses
In an "inaugural" State of the Union address, Presidents attempt to set the tone for a new administration.[29] Most of the rhetoric contained in early term speeches is forward-looking. In their first address, Presidents take positions on numerous policy issues in an attempt to direct the legislative agenda for the next four years. Since 1965, the median number of policy requests in a first year State of the Union address is 36.[30]

Midterm Addresses
State of the Union addresses in a President's second and third year of his term in office usually adopt a different tone. Presidents use a greater portion of their time in the address highlighting their policy achievements; approximately 10% of the sentences in mid-term addresses are credit-claiming statements. The number of policy requests typically decreases in a midterm speech, falling to a median of 30.[31]

Election Year Addresses
An impending election can influence the types of arguments Presidents make in their annual address. Claims of past achievements rise to 13% of the sentences. Policy proposals also rise to a median of 36 requests, perhaps in an attempt to demonstrate an active agenda if elected to a second term. Despite electoral considerations, Presidents do not use the State of the Union address to stump for office, according to scholars. If the election is mentioned at all, it is discussed indirectly and with a bipartisan tone.[32]

Second Term Addresses
The second term addresses of Presidents have disparate qualities. For example, President Reagan decreased both his credit claiming and policy proposals in his second-term addresses. On the other hand, President Clinton increased his policy proposals, while maintaining the same level of credit claiming. One characteristic, however, is common in second term addresses. In their second terms, Presidents concentrate more of their legislative requests on

defense and foreign policy.[33] It might be that Presidents turn towards building their legacy in their second terms of office and decide to focus more of their resources, political capital, and time on issues concerning defense and foreign policy.

Legislative Success and Policy Proposals

Given the powerful spotlight the State of the Union address provides for the President in his legislative role, a good question to ask is whether the proposals mentioned in the speech actually get enacted in the subsequent year. According to data from 1965 to 2002, on average, 43.3% of all policy proposals contained in a State of the Union address are enacted by Congress in the legislative session in which the President gave his speech, although the rate of legislative success varies widely throughout this time period.[34]

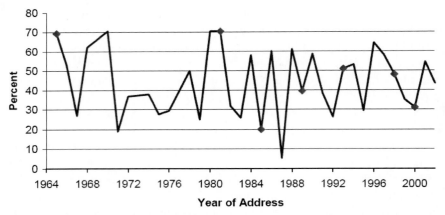

Source: Legislative Proposal Success Rate data provided by Hoffman and Howard, Addressing the State of the Union, p. 144.
Note: Data points with a marker indicate postelection addresses.

Figure 2. Legislative Proposal Success Rate. State of the Union Addresses, 1965-2002.

One pattern that can be discerned from **Figure 2** is that Presidents typically experience increased legislative success in the year immediately following an election. Of the five Presidents since 1965[35] who gave State of the Union postelection addresses, the average State of the Union legislative success rate was 51.4%, approximately eight percentage points higher than the overall average. The success rate falls for second-term addresses to 38.6%.[36]

Another comparison can be drawn between the legislative success rate during years of unified party government versus divided party government. The average legislative success rate during years of divided government is 40.9%. During years of unified government, the average legislative success rate rises to 49.3%.[37]

Capturing and Holding the Public's Attention

Evidence also suggests that Presidents can successfully capture the public's attention by mentioning a policy proposal in the State of the Union. Increased emphasis in a State of the Union speech translates into a higher level of public interest in that particular policy area. Both substantive arguments (in which the President took a position on an issue) and symbolic rhetoric (in which the President spoke generally about an issue but did not offer a specific recommendation) can increase public attention. Merely mentioning an issue in the State of the Union has the power to heighten the public's awareness of it. In a 2004 analysis of State of the Union addresses from 1946 to 2003, every 50 words a President devoted to an issue resulted in a 2% increase in the public identifying that problem as the most important in the nation.[38]

However, the President's ability to maintain the public's interest varies according to issue area. Increased public attention to economic policies mentioned by the President in his State of the Union address tends to evaporate by the end of the year. Conversely, however, the American public appears to retain its interest in foreign policy: attention to foreign policy issues mentioned by the President in his annual speech remains steady at the year's conclusion. It therefore seems reasonable to conclude that the President can use the State of the Union address more successfully to reshape and reconstitute public opinion about foreign policy.[39]

The empirical evidence suggests that presidents have used the address to discuss foreign policy issues in recent years. Using a "word cloud" tool that counts the frequency of words in a document, President George W. Bush said "terrorist" 14 times on September 20, 2001. In 2003, he used the name "Saddam Hussein" 19 times. In 2005, President Bush used the word "security" 29 times. "Iraq" was spoken 10 times in 2007. The frequent use of foreign policy terms is not, however, a product of a post-September 11 world. President Jimmy Carter said the word "Soviet" 57 times in his 1980 State of the Union, and President Lyndon Johnson said "Vietnam" 32 times in his 1966 speech.[40]

Given that Presidents now must compete with cable television channels not airing the State of the Union address, the threat of a declining viewership might depress the speech's potential salience.[41] Smaller viewing audiences do not, however, necessarily mean the annual speech is less influential. Many citizens rely upon media coverage of the State of the Union address to learn about the President's policy priorities. Research shows that media coverage of the State of the Union address leads to increased public knowledge about the highlighted issues, regardless of a person's educational background, age, or partisan affiliation.[42] Presidents have recently turned to the Internet as an alternative method of dissemination. In 2013, President Obama featured an "enhanced broadcast" of the State of the Union, which included charts and graphs on the White House website that appeared simultaneously as he spoke.[43] Even if an individual does not watch the address on television or the Internet, the State of the Union presents a significant opportunity for the President to communicate his ideological preferences, ideals, and policy agenda to the public writ large.

OPPOSITION RESPONSE

An opposition response is a speech given by select members of the political party not currently occupying the White House. The opposition response is usually broadcast immediately after the completion of the President's State of the Union address. It is a much shorter speech than the State of the Union; recent opposition responses have been approximately 1,500 words in length and lasted about 10 minutes. The practice of an opposition response to the State of the Union address began in 1966 when Senator Everett Dirksen and Representative Gerald Ford provided the Republican reply to President Lyndon Johnson.

Format

From 1967 to 1986, the opposition response adopted a variety of formats. Several times, the opposition response included comments from one or more Members of Congress. For example, in 1970, seven Democratic Members participated in a 45-minute televised response to President Richard Nixon's

State of the Union speech. In 1984, 12 Democratic Members recorded a reply to President Ronald Reagan's speech that was aired on most networks. In other instances, one or two Members delivered their party's official reply.[44]

By 1987, the opposition response adopted a format in which either one or two individuals provided a reply to the President's address. Parties often select rising stars, new congressional leaders, or possible presidential candidates to give the opposing view. For example, Senator Robert Dole gave the opposition response in 1996. The new Senate minority leader, Harry Reid, used the opposition response to introduce himself to the American people in 2005. In 2006, in an attempt to highlight Virginia's status as a well-managed state, the Democrats chose Governor Tim Kaine to give the reply.[45] In 2012, Indiana Governor Mitch Daniels, also considered to be an effective state chief executive, delivered the Republican response.[46]

In 1995, Republican Governor Christine Todd Whitman of New Jersey became the first non-congressional elected official to deliver the opposition response.[47] In 2007, Senator Jim Webb was the first freshman Member of Congress to provide the opposition response to the State of the Union address.

Common Rhetorical Arguments

No matter which party is giving the speech, opposition responses to the State of the Union address typically contain similar themes or arguments. The opposition's response routinely contains the following three rhetorical elements:

Call for Bipartisanship
As with the President in the State of the Union address, the opposition often calls for bipartisanship. Cooperation and consensus are common themes. Providing commentary from outside of the nation's capital, bipartisanship can play a more prominent role if a governor gives the address rather than a Member of Congress. For example, Democratic Governor Kathleen Sebelius of Kansas emphasized bipartisanship in her 2008 response. She stated:

> I'm a Democrat, but tonight, it doesn't really matter whether you think of yourself as a Democrat or a Republican or an Independent. Or none of the above.... And, so, I want to take a slight detour from tradition on this State of the Union night. In this time, normally reserved for the partisan response, I hope to offer you something more: An American Response.[48]

In other instances, the opposition response may ask the President directly to work in a bipartisan fashion to accomplish a particular task. In 2011, Representative Paul Ryan began his speech with prayers for the recovery of Representative Gabrielle Giffords and those injured or killed in the Tucson shooting massacre.

The Opposition' s Agenda

The political party not occupying the White House uses the opposition response to outline its policy agenda. While the President's State of the Union address can include a long list of proposals, the opposition response usually focuses on two or three major issues. The brevity of the opposition response limits the range of discussion. In 2007, Senator Jim Webb remarked, "It would not be possible in this short amount of time to actually rebut the President's message, nor would it be useful."[49] Opposition responses have always included a discussion of domestic issues. From time to time, the response also discusses foreign policy.

The response usually explains what the policy agenda would be if the opposition party controlled the White House. It may also include a discussion of issues that the President did not address in his State of the Union speech. A clear distinction is drawn between the President's priorities and the priorities of the opposing political party. For example, in his 2006 speech, Virginia Governor Tim Kaine repeated the phrase "There's a better way" six times during his televised address.[50]

Direct Response to President

The opposition often responds directly to specific proposals contained in the President's State of the Union address. Excerpts of the State of the Union address are usually leaked hours prior to delivery. This enables the opposing party to change its response by adding specific ripostes to the President's proposals. Other details are added as the President delivers his speech. For example, in 2000, Senator Bill Frist criticized the health care proposals offered by President Clinton:

> Earlier tonight we heard the President talk about his latest health care proposals. The last time he proposed a health plan was seven years ago ... Now tonight, 84 months later, the President has unveiled a similar plan just as bad as the first. It makes government even bigger and more bloated because each new program we heard about tonight—and there were about 11 of them in health care alone—comes with its own massive bureaucracy.[51]

Arguments directly responding to specific State of the Union policy proposals are usually criticisms of the President's approach or priorities. After such criticism, the opposition response usually offers counterproposals for the public's consideration.

Social Media

In his 2010 opposition response, Virginia Governor Bob McDonnell included an invitation for listeners to contribute ideas on social networking websites. He stated,

> In fact, many of our proposals are available online at solutions.gop.gov, and we welcome your ideas on Facebook and Twitter.[52]

This remark is the first request for listeners of a State of the Union Address or opposition response to use social media to communicate thoughts, ideas, or reactions.

CONCLUSION

The State of the Union address is an important weapon in the President's arsenal as a legislative leader. Although recent State of the Union addresses utilize common structure and often include similar types of arguments, the speech provides the President with the opportunity to outline his own policy agenda for the upcoming congressional session.

Presidents have two audiences in mind: Congress and the American public. Presidents must receive the support of a majority in the House, and oftentimes a supermajority in the Senate, to enact their legislative proposals. Presidents have realized that the American people can help accomplish this frequently difficult task. By appealing directly to the public, a President can use popular leverage to convince Congress to adopt his policy agenda. A campaign of such sustained public pressure must go beyond the State of the Union address, but Presidents often use the State of the Union as an initial vehicle to introduce policy priorities to a large viewing audience.

While the State of the Union address highlights the President's legislative role, it also serves as an annual reminder that the chief executive exists within a separated powers system. Legislative powers are shared between Congress and the presidency, evidenced by the constitutional requirement that the

President "shall from time to time give to the Congress Information of the State of the Union, and recommend to their Consideration such Measures as he shall judge necessary and expedient."

End Notes

[1] Clinton Rossiter, *The American Presidency* (New York: Harcourt, Brace, and Company, 1956).

[2] On this point, for more detail, see Ryan L Teten, "We the People: The Modern Rhetorical Popular Address of the Presidents during the Founding Period," *Political Research Quarterly*, vol. 60, no. 4 (December 2007), pp. 669-682.

[3] John Woolley and Gerhard Peters, The American Presidency Project, "Length of the State of the Union Addresses and Messages," at http://www.presidency accessed December 14, 2008.

[4] Gerhard Peters and John T. Woolley, "The State of the Union Address and the Rise of Rhetorical Leadership," in *State of the Union*, ed. Deborah Kalb, Gerhard Peters, and John T. Woolley (Washington: CQ Press, 2007), p. 2.

[5] Ryan L. Teten, "Evolution of the Modern Rhetorical Presidency: Presidential Presentation and Development of the State of the Union Address," *Presidential Studies Quarterly*, vol. 33, no. 2 (June 2003), p. 337.

[6] Gerhard Casper, "Executive-Congressional Separation of Power during the Presidency of Thomas Jefferson," *Stanford Law Review*, vol. 47, no. 3 (February 1995), p. 480.

[7] Chad Murphy, "The Evolution of the Modern Rhetorical Presidency: A Critical Response," *Presidential Studies Quarterly*, vol. 38, no. 2 (June 2008), pp. 303-306.

[8] Robert Alexander Kraig, *Woodrow Wilson and the Lost World of the Oratorical Statesman* (College Station, TX: Texas A&M University Press, 2004), p. 131.

[9] Several addresses made before a joint session of Congress were not technically titled as State of the Union Addresses. These speeches immediately followed a President's first term inauguration, and included Reagan's 1981 address, George H.W. Bush's 1989 address, Bill Clinton's 1993 address, George W. Bush's 2001 address, and Barack Obama's 2009 address. However, scholars consider these speeches to serve the same ceremonial, rhetorical, and political function as a typical State of the Union. Therefore, they are routinely counted and analyzed with the other Annual Addresses as such.

[10] The American Presidency Project, "Length of the State of the Union Messages and Addresses (in words)," at http://www.presidency

[11] Teten, *Evolution of the Modern Rhetorical Presidency*, p. 338.

[12] For example, H.Con.Res. 282, 110th Cong., 2nd sess.

[13] Interview with William Sims, Director of Chamber Security, House Sergeant at Arms, December 22, 2008.

[14] "State of the Union Address," at http://artandhistory.house.gov/house_history. http://clerk.house.gov/art_history/house_history/stateunion.html

[15] "Udall Urges Congress to Put Aside Partisan Divisions – Sit Together During State of the Union," available at http://markudall.senate.gov/?p=press_release&id=877, accessed on December 29, 2011.

[16] Interview with William Sims, December 22, 2008.

[17] Peters and Woolley, *State of the Union*, p. 11. Lenny Skutnik was a government employee who dived into the Potomac River to rescue a survivor after a plane departing from

Washington's National Airport crashed into the 14th Street Bridge. Reagan stated that Skutnik embodied "the spirit of American heroism at its finest."

[18] Charles A. Beard, *American Government and Politics*, 7th ed. (New York: Macmillan, 1935), p. 185.

[19] Karlyn Kohrs Campbell and Kathleen Hall Jamieson, *Presidents Creating the Presidency: Deeds Done in Words* (Chicago and London: University of Chicago Press, 2008), p. 139.

[20] John F. Kennedy, "Address to Congress on the State of the Union: January 11, 1962," in *State of the Union: Presidential Rhetoric from Woodrow Wilson to George W. Bush*, p. 577.

[21] Ronald Reagan, "Address before a Joint Session of Congress on the State of the Union," in *State of the Union: Presidential Rhetoric from Woodrow Wilson to George W. Bush*, p. 882.

[22] Matthew Esbaugh-Soha and Brandon Rottinghaus, "Presidential Position Taking and the Puzzle of Representation," *Presidential Studies Quarterly*, vol. 43, no. 1 (March 2013), pp. 1-15.

[23] George W. Bush, "Address before a Joint Session of Congress on the State of the Union," in *State of the Union*, p. 1083.

[24] Campbell and Jamieson, *Presidents Creating the Presidency*, p. 140.

[25] Franklin D. Roosevelt, "State of the Union Address," in *State of the Union*, p. 306.

[26] Campbell and Jamieson, *Presidents Creating the Presidency*, p. 141.

[27] Donna R. Hoffman and Alison D. Howard, *Addressing the State of the Union: The Evolution and Impact of the President's Big Speech* (Boulder: Lynne Rienner Publishers, 2006), p. 96.

[28] Ibid. p. 111. The median is used instead of the arithmetic mean (average) due to the presence of outliers in the data. The median is the middle value of a dataset. With outliers, such as Clinton in 2000 (87 policy requests) and Carter in 1980 (9 policy requests) the median more accurately represents the central tendency of the data.

[29] Ibid.

[30] The calculation is based upon data provided by Hoffman and Howard on p. 111. It does not include addresses given by Presidents Nixon, Ford, or Carter. These three Presidents declined to give a policy address to a joint session of Congress during their first year in office.

[31] Hoffman and Howard, *Addressing the State of the Union*, p. 115.

[32] Ibid. p. 116.

[33] Ibid. p. 119.

[34] Ibid. p. 143.

[35] The seven addresses analyzed are Johnson (1965), Reagan (1981), Reagan (1985), George H.W. Bush (1989), Clinton (1993), Clinton (1997), George W. Bush (2001).

[36] Hoffman and Howard, *Addressing the State of the Union*, pp. 145-146.

[37] Data provided by Hoffman and Howard, *Addressing the State of the Union*, pp. 144. Calculations provided by the authors. The number of SOTU addresses analyzed for divided government was 24; the number of SOTU addresses analyzed for unified government was 11.

[38] Adam B. Lawrence, "Does It Matter What Presidents Say? The Influence of Presidential Rhetoric on the Public Agenda, 1946-2003", (Ph.D. diss., University of Pittsburgh, 2004).

[39] Jeffrey E. Cohen, "Presidential Rhetoric and the Public Agenda," *American Journal of Political Science*, vol. 39, no. 1 (February 1995), pp. 95-100, at http://www.jstor.org/stable/info/2111759.

[40] The State of the Union word cloud tool can be accessed at http://stateoftheunion.onetwothree.net/index.shtml#. For an online tool that compares

speeches from 1934 through 2013, see http://graphics.wsj.com/SOTUWORDS2013/ #selCat=sCat1&l=2009&r=2013.

[41] Reed L. Welch, "Is Anybody Watching? The Audience for Televised Presidential Addresses," *Congress and the Presidency*, vol. 27, issue 1, (2000), pp. 41-58. According to media reports, President George W. Bush's final State of the Union address in 2008 drew 25 million viewers. This number was considerably less than 2007, when his speech drew 31 million viewers.

[42] Jason Barabas, "Presidential Policy Initiatives: How the Public Learns about State of the Union Proposals from the Mass Media," *Presidential Studies Quarterly*, vol. 38, no. 2 (June 2008), p. 215.

[43] See http://www.whitehouse.gov/state

[44] "State of the Union Address," at http://artandhistory.house.gov/house_history.

[45] The rankings were issued by the Government Performance Project of the Pew Center's on the States. See "Grading the States," ("Virginia Gets Top Grade in Management,") at http://www.pewstates.org/research/reports/grading-   (http://www.vaexcels.governor accessed on December 29, 2008.)

[46] The American Presidency Project, List of Opposition Responses to State of the Union Addresses at http://www.presidency

[47] Other governors, such as Bob Graham from Florida (1985), Bill Clinton from Arkansas (1985), and Charles Robb from Virginia (1986) participated in opposition responses, but were accompanied by several Members of Congress.

[48] "Transcript: Democratic Response," at http://www.cbsnews.com/stories/2008/01/28/politics accessed on December 29, 2008.

[49] "Transcript: Democratic Response," at http://www.cbsnews.com/stories/2007/01/23/politics accessed on December 30, 2008.

[50] "Virginia Governor Tim Kaine's Response," at http://www.washingtonpost.com/wp-dyn/content/article/2006/01/31/ AR2006013101246_pf.html, accessed on December 30, 2008.

[51] "Sen. Bill Frist," at http://www.pbs.org/newshour/bb/white_house/jan-june00/frist_1-27.html, accessed on December 30, 2008.

[52] "Bob McDonnell's GOP Response: Full Text," at http://www.cbsnews.com/stories/2010/01/27 /politics main6148483.shtml, accessed on October 28, 2010.

In: Federal Speeches: Policy and Practices   ISBN: 978-1-61761-755-3
Editor: Kathleen Weldon   © 2014 Nova Science Publishers, Inc.

Chapter 2

SPECIAL ORDER SPEECHES AND OTHER FORMS OF NON-LEGISLATIVE DEBATE IN THE HOUSE[*]

Judy Schneider

SUMMARY

Rules in the House of Representatives typically limit the time allowed for floor speeches and require debate to be germane to pending business. A series of unanimous consent practices have evolved that permit Members to address the House for specified durations and at specified times on subjects of their own choosing, outside the consideration of legislative business. The principal forms of such *non-legislative debate* are *special order speeches, one-minute speeches,* and *morning hour debates.*

BACKGROUND

Nearly every aspect of House floor proceedings is governed by time limitations. The Hour Rule for debate in the House, the five-minute rule for debate of amendments in the Committee of the Whole, and time limits

---

[*] This is an edited, reformatted and augmented version of Congressional Research Service Publication, No. RS21174, dated November 26, 2012.

imposed by special rules or under suspension of the rules procedures are essential tools for managing a crowded agenda in a large legislative body. In addition, Members in debate must confine themselves to the question under consideration. Together, these constraints severely limit the opportunities for Members to speak on other subjects of concern to them when legislation is being considered.

In response to this dilemma, several practices and procedures for "non-legislative debate" have evolved, to afford Members the opportunity to make themselves heard from the House floor on issues of interest. None of these practices is officially provided for in House rules. Rather, they are customs that have evolved as unanimous consent practices.

Unfettered by normal House germaneness requirements, Members using these forms of non-legislative debate can speak on a wide variety of subjects. Topics may include local, national, or international issues; proposed bills; or internal House procedures, as well as tributes or eulogies. In recent years, non-legislative debates have provided a convenient forum for Members, particularly the minority party, to draw attention to their legislative agenda.

The policies governing these practices have evolved over time in response to contemporary needs. Typically, on the opening day of a new Congress, unanimous consent agreements and the Speaker's announced policies governing the conduct of non-legislative debate during that Congress are stated. The practices prescribed for the 112th Congress are set out below.[1]

SPECIAL ORDER SPEECHES

Special order speeches occur routinely at the end of the day when all legislative business has been completed. Members may be recognized to speak on any topic they wish for up to 60 minutes. Recognition for special orders is the prerogative of the Speaker, and Members reserve their time in advance through their party's leadership. When recognizing a Member, the Speaker would say:

> Under a previous order of the House, the gentleman from _____ is recognized.

During the special order period, each party may first recognize a Member to speak for one hour. Then Members wishing to use a 30 minute block are recognized, with recognition alternating between the parties. It is common for each party's leadership to designate a Member to deliver a so-called "leadership special order" at some time during a special order period.

Pursuant to the Speaker's announced policy for the 112th Congress, up to four hours of special order speeches may be delivered, but in no case may the speeches extend beyond 10 p.m. The Member serving as the presiding officer, following consultation with the leadership and notification to the House, may extend the four-hour period for special orders on a given day, but not beyond 10 p.m.

The time allotted each day is divided equally between the parties, and initial and subsequent recognition alternates between the majority and minority. For more detailed information, see CRS Report RL30136, *Special Order Speeches: Current House Practices*, by Judy Schneider.

ONE-MINUTE SPEECHES

One-minute speeches are typically given at the start of the legislative day, but may occur at other times in the legislative program, including the end of the day. Customarily, after the daily prayer, the Pledge of Allegiance, and approval of the previous day's *Journal*, Members ask for unanimous consent to address the House for one minute on a topic of their choice. When seeking recognition, a Member would say:

> I ask unanimous consent to address the House for one minute and to revise and extend my remarks.

Recognition for one-minute speeches is at the prerogative of the Speaker, who may limit daily speeches to a certain number, or move them to a different place in the program, on any given day. Members seeking recognition for this purpose sit in the first row on their party's side of the chamber. Recognition for one-minute speeches alternates between the majority and the minority, with possible exceptions for Members representing the leadership, and Members having business requests.

For more detailed information, see CRS Report RL30135, *One-Minute Speeches: Current House Practices*, by Judy Schneider.

MORNING HOUR DEBATES

Since the 103rd Congress, the House, by unanimous consent, has set aside a period on Mondays and Tuesdays for the purpose of conducting "morning hour debates." The amount of time reserved for these speeches varies. In the 112th Congress, the House has agreed to two different schedules for morning hour debate. Before February 1, 2011, the House could convene on Mondays and Tuesdays for special order speeches two hours before the regular House meeting times. After February 1, 2011, the House may convene for morning hour speeches on Monday, Tuesday, Wednesday, and Thursday, two hours before the regular meeting time. The House may also meet at a time different from the regular meeting times for the 112th Congress established by H.Res. 10, by adopting a resolution for that purpose.

The two hour period for morning hour speeches will be divided between the two parties. Members must reserve time in advance with their respective leadership, and speeches are limited to five minutes. More time may be granted for speeches by the majority leader, the minority leader, and the minority whip. The chair alternates initial and subsequent recognition between the majority and minority parties, in accord with lists supplied by the leadership. When recognizing Members for this purpose, the Speaker would say:

> Pursuant to the order of the House of [date here] the Chair will now recognize Members from lists submitted by the majority and minority leaders for morning-hour debate. The Chair will alternate recognition between the parties, with each Member, other than the majority and minority leaders and the minority whip, limited to 5 minutes.

When morning hour debate is concluded, the House recesses until the meeting time established for that day's session. Morning hour debate must conclude at least 10 minutes before the scheduled regular meeting time for the day's session.

End Note

[1] The procedures governing extra-legislative debate are available in the *Congressional Record*. "Making in Order Morning-Hour Debate," remarks in House, *Congressional Record*, daily edition, January 5, 2011, pp. H28-H31. The rules for the 112th Congress are in *The Constitution, Jefferson's Manual, and Rules of the House of Representatives*, H.Doc. 111-

157, 111th Cong., 2nd sess., [compiled by] John V. Sullivan, Parliamentarian (Washington: GPO, 2011).

In: Federal Speeches: Policy and Practices   ISBN: 978-1-61761-755-3
Editor: Kathleen Weldon   © 2014 Nova Science Publishers, Inc.

Chapter 3

SPECIAL ORDER SPEECHES: CURRENT HOUSE PRACTICES[*]

Judy Schneider

SUMMARY

Special order speeches (commonly called "special orders") usually take place at the end of the day after the House has completed all legislative business. During the special order period, individual Representatives deliver speeches on topics of their choice for up to 60 minutes. Special orders provide one of the few opportunities for non-legislative debate in the House. They also give Members a chance to speak outside the time restrictions that govern legislative debate in the House and the Committee of the Whole.

The rules of the House do not provide for special order speeches. Instead, special orders have evolved as a *unanimous consent practice* of the House. Recognition for special orders is the prerogative of the Speaker. During the special order period, Members must abide by the rules of the House, the chamber's precedents, and the "Speaker's announced policies," in that order. The term "Speaker's announced policies" refers to the Speaker's policies on certain aspects of House procedure.

In practice, the Speaker's current policies on special orders (announced on January 6, 2009) govern recognition for special order

---

[*] This is an edited, reformatted and augmented version of Congressional Research Service Publication, No. RL30136, dated January 31, 2013.

speeches as well as the reservation and television broadcast of these speeches. Under these announced policies, there are generally three "stages" to each day's special order period:

- first, five-minute special orders by *individual Members*;
- next, special orders longer than five minutes (normally 60 minutes in length) by *the party's leadership or a designee*; and
- last, special orders longer than five minutes (length varies from 6 to 60 minutes) by *individual Members.*

Members usually reserve special orders in advance through their party's leadership. Instead of delivering a special order speech on the House floor, Members may choose to insert their speech in either the House pages of the *Congressional Record* or the section known as the "Extensions of Remarks."

Reform proposals were advanced in recent Congresses to address both concerns about breaches in decorum during special order speeches and the costs of conducting these speeches.

INTRODUCTION

Special order speeches (commonly called "special orders") usually take place at the end of the day after the House of Representatives has completed all legislative business. During the special order period, individual Representatives can deliver speeches on topics of their choice for up to 60 minutes. Special order speeches give Members a chance to speak outside the time restrictions that govern legislative debate in the House and the Committee of the Whole. These speeches also provide one of the few opportunities for non-legislative debate in the House,[1] where debate is almost always confined to pending legislative business.[2]

This report examines current House practices for reserving special order speeches and securing recognition for these speeches. Differences between *inserted* and *delivered* special orders, various uses of special orders, and current reform proposals are also discussed.

GOVERNING AUTHORITIES

The rules of the House do not provide for special order speeches. Instead, special orders have evolved as a *unanimous consent practice* of the House.

While any Member can object to the practice of holding daily special order speeches, this happens infrequently.

During the special order period, Members must abide by the rules of the House, the chamber's precedents, and the "Speaker's announced policies," in that order. Relevant House rules include those governing debate, decorum, and the Speaker's power of recognition. For example, a Representative cannot deliver a special order longer than 60 minutes because this would violate House Rule XVII, clause 2, which limits individual Members to "one hour in debate on any question." When a Member's 60-minute special order expires, he cannot even ask unanimous consent to address the House for an additional minute.[3]

He can speak again, however, if time is yielded under another Representative's special order. Individual Representatives with reserved special order speeches will commonly yield time to colleagues during the speech.

House precedents discuss how the chamber has interpreted and applied its rules. These precedents are published in several parliamentary reference publications.[4] Under House precedents, for example, individual Members cannot deliver more than one special order each legislative day.[5]

The term "Speaker's announced policies" refers to the Speaker's policies on certain aspects of House procedure (e.g., decorum in debate, conduct of electronic votes, recognition for special orders). These policies are usually announced on the opening day of a new Congress. In practice, the Speaker's current policies on special orders (announced on January 3, 2013) govern recognition for special order speeches and the reservation and television broadcast of these speeches.[6]

Recognition for Special Orders

Recognition for special orders is the prerogative of the Speaker. While special orders routinely begin once legislative business is completed, the Speaker is not required to recognize Members for special orders as soon as legislative business ends.

Under his power of recognition (House Rule XVII, clause 2), the Speaker can first recognize other Members for "unanimous-consent requests and permissible motions."[7]

The Speaker may also interrupt or reschedule the special order period to proceed to legislative or other business. Moreover, the Speaker can recognize

Representatives for special orders earlier in the day (e.g., when the House plans to consider major legislation through the evening hours).

A majority party Representative appointed as "Speaker pro tempore" usually presides in the chair during special-orders. In recognizing Members, the chair observes the following announced policies of the Speaker:

- Representatives are first recognized for five-minute special order speeches, and then for longer speeches that do not exceed 60 minutes.
- Recognition alternates between the majority and minority for both the *initial* special order and *subsequent* special orders in each time category (i.e., five-minute special orders; longer special orders). In recognizing individual Members, the chair follows the order specified in the list of special order requests submitted by each party's leadership (see "Reservation of Special Orders" section).
- No special orders are allowed after midnight *on any day.*
- *On Tuesdays,* after all legislative business is completed, the chair can recognize Members for five-minute special orders and unlimited longer special orders until midnight.
- *On every day but Tuesday,* after the five-minute special orders, the chair can recognize Members for no more than four hours of longer special orders.[8] The four hours are divided equally between the majority and minority. Each party can reserve the first hour of longer special orders for its leadership or a designee (a so-called "leadership special order"—see below for more information). When less than four hours remains until midnight, each party's two-hour period is prorated.[9]

Each party's leadership usually chooses a designee to deliver a leadership special order during the party's first hour of longer special orders.[10] This designee will sometimes lead a thematic special order and yield time to other party Members.

For example, on May 7, 1997, the minority leader's designee delivered a 60-minute special order on H.R. 3 (juvenile crime control legislation), with participation from other Democratic Members.[11] The majority leader's designee then led a 60- minute special order on the 1997 balanced budget agreement, during which he yielded time to other Republican Members.[12]

To summarize, under the Speaker's current announced policies, there are generally three "stages" to each day's special order period:

- first, five-minute special orders by *individual Members*;
- next, special orders longer than five minutes (normally 60 minutes in length) by *the party's leadership or designee*; and
- last, special orders longer than five minutes (length varies from six to 60 minutes) by *individual Members*.

RESERVATION OF SPECIAL ORDERS

Members reserve five-minute and longer special orders through their party leadership: *Democratic* Members reserve time through the Office of the Majority Leader, and *Republican* Members reserve time through the Republican cloakroom or the party leadership desk on the House floor. Under the Speaker's announced policies, Members cannot reserve special orders more than one week in advance.

Moreover, the date of the reservation does not affect the order in which the chair recognizes Members for special orders.[13]

The Speaker's announced policies require that the majority and minority leadership give the chair a list each day showing how the party's two hours of longer special orders will be allocated among party Members. The chair follows this list in recognizing Members for longer special orders.

For five-minute special orders, the majority and minority leadership compile a list of five-minute special order reservations each day. This list is given to a party Member who asks unanimous consent that each Member on the list be allowed to address the House for five minutes on a specific date. Permission is routinely granted by the House. A notice of granted five-minute special orders appears in the House section of the daily *Congressional Record* (under the heading "Special Orders Granted") and on the inside page of the daily "House Calendar" (formally called *Calendars of the United States House of Representatives and History of Legislation*).

Individual Members may also ask unanimous consent to give a special order speech at the last minute, to use another Representative's reserved special order time, or to deliver a reserved special order out of the established sequence for that day. These unanimous consent requests are made infrequently and permission is usually granted.

TELEVISION BROADCAST OF SPECIAL ORDERS

House Rule V places the broadcasting of House proceedings under the Speaker's exclusive direction. The Speaker's announced policies prohibit House-controlled television cameras from panning the chamber during special orders.[14] Instead, a caption (also known as a "crawl") appears at the bottom of the television screen indicating that legislative business has been completed and the House is proceeding with special orders.

INSERTED SPECIAL ORDERS

Instead of delivering a special order speech on the House floor, Members may insert their speech in either the House pages of the *Congressional Record* or the section known as the "Extensions of Remarks."[15]

Special orders inserted in the *House section* are published in a distinctive typeface alongside the special orders delivered that day on the House floor. Members must decide in advance to insert special orders in the *House section*. They make this decision when reserving the special order through their party's leadership. A Representative who wants to participate in another Member's reserved special order can also decide in advance to insert his remarks in the House section. This decision is coordinated with the Member holding the special order reservation. The Representative's inserted remarks appear in a distinctive typeface during the other Member's reserved special order.

Members who are not present when recognized for their special order speech routinely have the option of inserting this speech in the *Extensions of Remarks section*. Permission of the House is required to insert any material in this section. When the House grants unanimous consent to special order requests, it typically gives Representatives permission to "revise and extend" their remarks and to "include extraneous material." This permission is usually reported in the House pages of the *Congressional Record* under the heading "Special Orders Granted" (see above). Special order speeches inserted in the *Extensions of Remarks section* appear alongside other inserted material (e.g., legislative statements not delivered on the floor, newspaper articles, letters from constituents) and are not identified as special orders. All materials in the *Extensions of Remarks section* appear in a distinctive typeface.

DIFFERENCES BETWEEN INSERTED AND DELIVERED SPECIAL ORDERS

The practical difference between *inserting* and *delivering* a special order speech is twofold. First, inserted special orders are available only to readers of the hard copy and on-line versions of the *Congressional Record*. By contrast, special orders delivered on the House floor reach a larger audience through C-SPAN's televised coverage of House floor proceedings. Second, inserted special order speeches incur less cost than those delivered on the House floor. While both inserted and delivered special order involve *Congressional Record* printing costs, only delivered speeches entail the expenses of keeping the House in formal session (e.g., electricity, salaries of House officers and staff).

VARIOUS USES OF SPECIAL ORDERS

Members often use special orders to address subjects unrelated to legislation before the House. They deliver speeches on broad policy issues, a bill they have introduced, and local, national, or international events. They also present eulogies and tributes.

Special orders are also used to debate specific legislation and policy issues outside the time restrictions that govern legislative debate in the House and the Committee of the Whole. As mentioned earlier, each party's leadership sometimes reserves a 60-minute special order to present party views on a particular bill or policy issue. In addition, Members of both parties may coordinate their special orders to debate legislation. For example, in the 104th Congress, the two parties reserved consecutive, 60-minute special orders to conduct a "real give-and-take kind of debate" of H.J.Res. 159 (a proposed constitutional amendment to require two-thirds majorities for bills increasing taxes).[16] Majority and minority Members participated in each party's 60-minute special order. In a departure from regular practice, these special orders took place in the middle of the day before the House considered the joint resolution.

The special order period also provides a forum where Members can practice and hone their debate skills. Veteran Representatives have advised new Members, in particular, to reserve special orders for this purpose:

... before you participate in general debate on a bill ... get some practice. Get a special order and have a few of your friends participate with you. Get the feel of being in the well of the House, how the lectern can move up and down, how the microphones work. Practice in the somewhat stilted language of yielding to other colleagues and so forth, so that when you do get into the real legislative fight it isn't all new; you have a little bit of the feel of debating in the House.[17]

During special orders, freshmen majority Members also have an opportunity to gain experience presiding as "Speaker pro tempore."

EARLIER ANNOUNCED POLICIES OF THE SPEAKER

The Speaker's current announced policies on special orders build upon earlier policies, mainly those implemented on February 23, 1994.[18] These 1994 policies significantly changed special order procedures by imposing new restrictions (e.g., four-hour limitation on longer special orders, no special order reservations more than one week in advance). Before early 1994, special orders could be reserved months in advance and it was not unusual to have more than 10 hours of special orders reserved for a single day. Special order speeches also could be delivered after midnight and all-night special orders took place on occasion.

The Speaker's announced policies before 1994 required that Members be recognized for five-minute special order speeches first and then for longer speeches, and that recognition alternate between majority and minority Members.[19] When studying special order speeches before February 23, 1994, it is useful to remember these speeches were reserved and delivered under the Speaker's earlier, less restrictive policies.

BREACHES IN DECORUM

The House Rules Committee's Subcommittee on Rules and Organization of the House held hearings on April 17, 1997, and May 1, 1997, to discuss issues raised in *Civility in the House of Representatives* (hereafter referred to as *Civility*), a report prepared for the March 1997 bipartisan retreat of House Members.[20] *Civility* examined the public's perception of rising incivility in the

House and recommended actions to reduce this perception and actual breaches in decorum.

The report pointed out that incivility was more likely to take place during special orders and one-minute speeches than during other periods of House floor proceedings. According to *Civility*, unparliamentary language "that would be taken down in regular debate was more likely to be tolerated or 'cautioned'" during special orders.[21] The report attributed this situation to the low number of Members present during special orders—it was unlikely a Member would make a timely demand that unparliamentary words be taken down and, even if this demand was made, "it would be all but impossible to locate the Members needed to vote" on an appeal of the chair's ruling.[22] On this last point, the report recommended that the House change its rules to require that appealed rulings of the chair after regular business be voted on the next legislative day.[23] This rules change, the report argued, would encourage the chair to intervene more frequently against unparliamentary language in special orders.[24]

The 1999 report provided data on the 105th Congress generally, and the December 1998 impeachment debate specifically. No recommendations were included. The House Rules Committee held hearings on the 1999 report in April 1999.

COSTS

As discussed earlier, daily special orders entail *Congressional Record* printing expenses for delivered and inserted special orders and the costs of keeping the House in formal session for delivered special orders (e.g., electricity, salaries of House staff and officers).

On February 9, 1999, Representative Lynn Rivers (D-Mich.) introduced H.Res. 47, a resolution to amend House rules to require that "the expenses of special-order speeches be paid from the Members' Representational Allowances of Members making such speeches." Each Representative has a "Members' Representational Allowance" (MRA) for expenses related to official and representational duties (e.g., employment of staff, travel, franked mail, supplies). H.Res. 47 was referred to the House Committee on Rules upon introduction but did not receive committee action in the 106th Congress. Representative Rivers introduced identical resolutions (H.Res. 97) in the 105th Congress and (H.Res. 263) in the 104th Congress, but no action was taken on either measure.

End Notes

[1] One-minute speeches (usually every day) and morning hour debates (on Mondays and Tuesdays only) also provide opportunities for non-legislative debate, but only for one minute and five minutes, respectively.

[2] Under House Rule XVII, clause 1(b)(1), a Member "shall be confined to the question under debate" (almost always the legislative business before the House).

[3] U.S. Congress, House, *House Practice: A Guide to the Rules, Precedents and Procedures of the House*, 112th Cong., 1st sess. (Washington: GPO, 2011), "Consideration and Debate" chap. 16, sec. 50, p. 432.

[4] For more information, see CRS Report RL30787, *Parliamentary Reference Sources: House of Representatives*.

[5] *House Practice*, "Consideration and Debate" chap.16, sec. 50, p. 432.

[6] The full text of these announced policies of the Speaker appear in Congressional Record, daily edition, January 3, 2013, pp. H25-H27.

[7] U.S. Congress, House, *Procedure in the U.S. House of Representatives*, 97th Cong. (Washington: GPO, 1982), chap. 21, sec. 9.6-9.7, pp. 312-313.

[8] This four-hour limitation can only be extended if the chair grants permission after consultation with the leadership of both parties and notification to the House.

[9] For example, if the House completes legislative business at 11:00 p.m., Members are first recognized for five-minute special orders, and then the time remaining until midnight is divided between the two parties for longer special orders.

[10] On occasion, a party's leadership may designate two party Reps. to lead back-to-back special orders that collectively total one hour. For example, on July 14, 1996, Rep. Frank Pallone and Del. Eleanor Holmes Norton were recognized for separate 30-minute special orders as the minority leader's designees. See *Congressional Record*, daily edition, vol. 142, July 14, 1996, pp. H5036 and H5039.

[11] *Congressional Record*, daily edition, vol. 143, May 7, 1997, pp. H2338-H2343.

[12] Ibid., pp. H2343-H2348.

[13] This current practice, firmly established by the Speaker's announced policies of January 5, 1995, and extended by the announced policies of January 3, 2013, departs from earlier House practice. Previously, Members were recognized for special order speeches in the order that they reserved their speech (i.e., when three Members each reserved a 30-minute special order for a particular day, the Member who reserved the speech at the earliest date was recognized first). For other differences between current and earlier House practices, see the "Earlier Announced Policies of the Speaker" section.

[14] From 1984 to 1994, House-controlled television cameras panned the entire chamber during special orders.

[15] There are three sections in the daily *Congressional Record*: (1) the proceedings of the House; (2) the proceedings of the Senate; and (3) the "Extensions of Remarks," a section where Members of the House can insert "a speech that was not actually delivered on the floor" or "extraneous materials related to the subject under discussion," with the House's permission. *House Practice*, "Congressional Record" chap.15, sec. 5, pp. 377-379.

[16] See *Congressional Record*, daily edition, vol. 142, April 15, 1996, pp. H3240-H3256.

[17] Donald G. Tacheron and Morris K. Udall, *The Job of the Congressman*, 2nd ed. (Indianapolis: Bobbs-Merrill Company, 1970), pp. 208-209.

[18] These policies were announced on Feb. 11, 1994, and implemented on February 23, 1994, for a 90-day trial period. Their application was later extended for the duration of the 103rd Cong. See *Congressional Record*, daily edition, vol. 140, February 11, 1994, p. H542, and June 10, 1994, p. H4333.

[19] See *Congressional Record*, vol. 130, August 8, 1984, p. 22963.

[20] Kathleen Hall Jamieson, *Civility in the House of Representatives*, (Philadelphia: Annenberg Public Policy Center, 1997), 105 p. An updated version, covering the 105th Cong., was prepared in March 1999 for the 1999 Hershey retreat. Kathleen Hall Jamieson, *Civility in the House of Representatives* (Philadelphia: Annenberg Public Policy Center, 1999), 18 p.

[21] Ibid., p. 61.

[22] Ibid., p. 85. Also, for a discussion of the "taking down of words" procedure, see *House Practice*, "Consideration and Debate" chapter 16, sec. 28-32, pp. 408-412.

[23] Civility, p. 99.

[24] Ibid.

In: Federal Speeches: Policy and Practices   ISBN: 978-1-61761-755-3
Editor: Kathleen Weldon   © 2014 Nova Science Publishers, Inc.

Chapter 4

ONE-MINUTE SPEECHES: CURRENT HOUSE PRACTICES[*]

Judy Schneider

SUMMARY

Recognition for one-minute speeches (commonly called "one minutes") in the House of Representatives is the prerogative of the Speaker. A period for one minutes usually takes place at the beginning of the legislative day after the daily prayer, the Pledge of Allegiance, and approval of the previous day's *Journal*. During this time, Representatives ask unanimous consent to address the House for one minute on a topic of their choice. In addition, one-minute speeches are often permitted after legislative business ends, but before special order speeches begin.

The rules of the House do not provide for one-minute speeches. Instead, one minutes have evolved as a *unanimous consent practice* of the chamber. During one-minute speeches, Members must abide by the rules of the House, the chamber's precedents, and the "Speaker's announced policies," in that order. The term "Speaker's announced policies" refers to the Speaker's policies on certain aspects of House procedure, such as recognition for one minutes.

Representatives seeking recognition for one minutes sit in the first row on their party's side of the chamber. From the chair's vantage point, Republican Members sit on the left side of the chamber and Democratic

---

[*] This is an edited, reformatted and augmented version of Congressional Research Service Publication, No. RL30135, dated January 23, 2013.

Members on the right side. The chair moves from his right to left in recognizing Members on each side of the aisle. When recognized by the chair, individual Members ask unanimous consent to address the House for one minute and to revise and extend their remarks. Permission is almost always granted. Members deliver one-minute speeches from the well of the chamber. They are limited to one minute and cannot ask unanimous consent for additional time. Instead of delivering a one-minute speech on the House floor, a Member may ask unanimous consent to insert the speech in the House section of the *Congressional Record*.

Members need not reserve one-minute speeches in advance through their party's leadership. Nevertheless, the party leadership communication arms—known as the "Democratic Message Group" and the "Republican Theme Team"—sometimes coordinate party Members to deliver one minutes on the issue designated as the party's daily message. These party Members usually receive priority seating for recognition purposes.

INTRODUCTION

One-minute speeches (commonly called "one minutes") provide one of the few opportunities for non-legislative debate in the House, where debate is almost always confined to the pending legislative business.[1] Recognition for one-minute speeches is the prerogative of the Speaker. A period for one minutes usually takes place at the beginning of the legislative day after the daily prayer, the Pledge of Allegiance, and approval of the previous day's *Journal*.[2] During this time, Representatives ask unanimous consent to address the House for one minute on a topic of their choice. In addition, one minutes are often permitted after legislative business ends but before special order speeches begin.

This report examines current House practices governing recognition for one-minute speeches, the delivery of one minutes, and their insertion in the *Congressional Record*. Various uses of one minutes and reform proposals are also discussed.

GOVERNING AUTHORITIES

One-minute speeches are not provided for in the rules of the House. Instead, they have evolved as a *unanimous consent practice* of the chamber.

Members must ask unanimous consent to address the House for one minute (for more information, see "Delivering One-Minute Speeches," below).

During one-minute speeches, Members must abide by the rules of the House, the chamber's precedents, and the "Speaker's announced policies," in that order. Relevant House rules include those governing debate, decorum, and the Speaker's power of recognition. House precedents discuss how the chamber has interpreted and applied its rules.[3] Under House precedents, for example, individual Members can be recognized for a one-minute speech only once each legislative day.[4]

The term "Speaker's announced policies" refers to the Speaker's policies on certain aspects of House procedure, such as decorum in debate, the conduct of electronic votes, and recognition for one minutes and special orders. These policies are usually announced on the opening day of a new Congress. The Speaker's current policies on recognition for one minutes are those that were first announced on August 8, 1984. These policies have been followed in each succeeding Congress.[5]

RECOGNITION FOR ONE-MINUTE SPEECHES

Recognition for one-minute speeches is the prerogative of the Speaker. Under his power of recognition (House Rule XVII, clause 2), the Speaker decides when he will entertain unanimous consent requests to address the House for one minute, and how many one-minute speeches he will allow.

According to the Speaker's announced policies, the chair "reserves the right to limit one-minute speeches to a certain period of time or to a special place in the program on any given day, with notice to the leadership."[6] When pressing legislative business is before the House, the Speaker may decide to limit the number of one-minute speeches, to postpone one minutes until after legislative business, or to forego them altogether.

A period for one-minute speeches (hereafter referred to as "the one-minute speech period") usually takes place at the beginning of each legislative day after the daily prayer, the Pledge of Allegiance, and approval of the previous day's *Journal*. The Speaker determines the number of one minutes permitted during this period. This number varies from day to day. The Speaker might allow an unlimited number of speeches one day and then limit the number the following day (e.g., allow only 10 one minutes on each side of the aisle). The majority and minority leadership usually receive advance notification of any limitations.

A majority party Representative appointed as "Speaker *pro tempore*" usually presides in the chair during the one-minute speech period. In recent practice, the chair often announces how many one minutes will be allowed before the one-minute speech period begins.

Representatives seeking recognition for one minutes sit in the first row on their party's side of the chamber. From the chair's vantage point, Republican Members sit on the left side of the chamber and Democratic Members on the right side. In recognizing Members for one minutes, the chair observes the following announced policies of the Speaker:

> The chair will alternate recognition for one-minute speeches between majority and minority Members, in the order in which they seek recognition in the well under present practice from the Chair's right to the Chair's left, with possible exceptions for Members of the leadership and Members having business requests.[7]

Because the chair moves from his right to left in recognizing Members, the Republican Member seated closest to the center aisle is recognized first on the *Republican side*, and the Democratic Member seated closest to the Speaker's lobby is recognized first on the *Democratic side*. Recognition alternates from majority to minority throughout the period for one minutes.

In addition to the one-minute speech period, Members can usually ask unanimous consent to deliver a one minute after legislative business ends but before special order speeches begin.

COORDINATION ROLE OF PARTY LEADERSHIP

Members do not have to reserve one-minute speeches in advance through their party's leadership.[8] Nevertheless, the party leadership communication arms—known as the "Democratic Message Group" and the "Republican Theme Team"—sometimes coordinate party Members to deliver one minutes on the issue designated as the party's daily message. On days when the number of one-minute speeches is limited, these party Members usually receive priority seating for recognition purposes (i.e., on the right side of the party's first row). The daily message usually presents the party's views on specific legislation before the House or its position on a policy or political issue.

DELIVERING ONE-MINUTE SPEECHES

When recognized by the chair, individual Members ask unanimous consent to address the House for one minute and to revise and extend their remarks.[9] Permission is almost always granted. Members speak from the well of the chamber. They are limited to one minute and cannot ask unanimous consent for additional time. When the chair announces that one minute has expired, the Member can finish the sentence underway but must then stop speaking. The chair's calculation of time consumed during a one-minute speech "is not subject to challenge on a point of order."[10]

When Members cannot finish their remarks in one minute, the permission to extend allows them to complete their speech in writing in the *Congressional Record*. The undelivered portion of their speech appears in a distinctive typeface. Permission to extend also authorizes Members to insert extraneous material such as a newspaper article or a constituent letter during a one-minute speech. The inserted material appears in a distinctive typeface.

Joint Committee on Printing regulations for publication of the *Congressional Record* provide that "any extraneous matter included in any statement by a Member" be printed in the "Extensions of Remarks" section of the *Congressional Record* but noted in the Members' remarks.[11] This requirement is not always observed. A review of 10 one minutes containing extraneous matter from January to July 1997 found that in each case the extraneous matter was printed in the House section (not in the "Extensions of Remarks") of the *Congressional Record* along with the one-minute speech.

The Joint Committee on Printing's regulations also require that one-minute speeches longer than 300 words "delivered during the morning business" (i.e., during the one-minute speech period at the start of the day) be printed "following the business of the day." In practice, these one minutes usually appear in the House section of the *Congressional Record* immediately before the five-minute special orders.

INSERTING ONE-MINUTE SPEECHES

Instead of delivering a one-minute speech on the House floor, a Member may insert the speech in the House section of the *Congressional Record* alongside the one minutes delivered on the floor that day. The Representative asks unanimous consent to insert the one-minute speech in the *Congressional*

Record and yields back his time. The inserted speech is published in a distinctive typeface.

The practical difference between inserting and delivering a one-minute speech is the speech's audience. *Inserted* one minutes are available to readers of the hard copy and online versions of the *Congressional Record*. By contrast, *delivered* one minutes reach a larger audience through CSPAN's televised coverage of House floor proceedings.

Various Uses of One Minutes

The unrestricted content and short length of one-minute speeches make them an attractive communication tool for individual Members and the party leadership. In addition, the usual position of one minutes at the start of day means they can be covered by broadcast news organizations in time for evening news programs.

Individual Members often use one minutes to share information with colleagues such as announcing a new bill they have introduced or explaining a floor amendment they will offer later that day. In practice, these one minutes serve as a visual "Dear Colleague" letter. Representatives also use one-minute speeches to deliver eulogies and tributes concerning individuals and organizations in their congressional district. One minutes also provide Members with an opportunity to express their views on bills, policy issues, and local, national, and international events.

For junior Members, one-minute speeches provide a valuable debate opportunity. Representative Chabot highlighted this point in a 105th Congress one-minute speech on the importance of one minutes: "As my colleagues know, a freshman or sophomore Member might sit at a committee meeting for two hours before being able to pose one question to a witness. He or she, if lucky, might get 30 seconds to debate a pending bill on the floor. One-minute speeches give these Members and the people they represent back home a chance to be heard."[12]

Some Representatives have made one-minute speeches a regular part of their media and communication strategy. By delivering one minutes, they reach a national audience of C-SPAN television viewers and webcast users, including constituents. Some Members also disseminate their one-minute speeches through other channels, such as mailing constituents a copy of the speech printed in *Congressional Record* or providing local news organizations with a video press release.

As mentioned earlier, the Democratic Message Group and the Republican Theme Team sometimes use one-minute speeches as a vehicle for transmitting the party's daily message. The one-minute speech period provides a forum where different Members of the party can speak on the designated theme to a national audience. This use of one minutes has been criticized by some Representatives and congressional observers. During a 104th Congress special order speech on civility in the House, one Member stated that one minutes in the morning had "become theme-team efforts just to excite and aggravate, to get sound bites for television, rather than a healthy discourse on the issues."[13]

REFORM PROPOSALS

Breaches in decorum during one-minute speeches in the 104th and 105th Congresses have prompted some reform proposals that range from eliminating one minutes to postponing them until the completion of legislative business. These proposals have been advanced in letters to the Speaker, in testimony at congressional hearings, and in the *Civility in the House of Representatives* report that was prepared for the March 1997 bipartisan retreat of House Members. The 1999 report updated the data for the 105th Congress but did not contain recommendations.[14]

LETTERS TO THE SPEAKER

In August 1996, Representative Archer and former Representative Beilenson sent a letter to the Speaker urging him to stop recognizing Members for one-minute speeches at the start of the day. Signed by a bipartisan group of 50 Members, the letter proposed that one minutes only be permitted after the completion of legislative business. The letter noted that one minutes had increasingly become "a series of sound-bite assaults often prepared not by Members themselves, but by Republican and Democratic political staff who have found this format to be highly conducive to the kinds of attacks that used to be reserved for campaign commercials."[15] Postponing one minutes until after legislative business, the letter's signatories argued, would reduce this manner of using one minutes.

On September 5, 1996, the proposal in the letter was discussed at a joint hearing of the two subcommittees of the House Rules Committee.

Representative Archer testified that "Partisan and poisonous 1-minute speeches unfavorably set the tone for our legislative business.... If we move 1-minutes to the conclusion of the day, Members will be less inclined to focus on the negative, politically charged messages, and 1-minutes would once again turn to their original positive intent."[16] In separate testimony, Representative Beilenson noted that one-minute speeches "often contain purposefully written, catchy phrases that make good sound bites." Moving one minutes to the end of the day, he argued, would "negate their usefulness to news operations" and remove the incentive to envelop one-minute speeches in sound bites.[17]

At the start of the 105th Congress, a letter advancing the same reform proposal was sent to the Speaker and to the minority leader by Representatives Archer and Hamilton. A bipartisan group of 59 Members signed the letter. A similar letter was circulated in the 106th Congress.

CIVILITY IN THE HOUSE OF REPRESENTATIVES REPORT

Civility in the House of Representatives (hereafter referred to as *Civility*) examined the public's perception of rising incivility in the House and suggested ways to reduce both this perception and actual breaches in decorum. The report point out that incivility was more likely to take place during one-minute and special order speeches than during other periods of House floor proceedings.

Civility recommended that the House either eliminate one-minute speeches or move these speeches to another time of the day (i.e., to a time other than the start of the day). Holding one minutes in the morning, the report argued, "can set a hostile tone for debate."[18] The report noted the "advent of theme teams" and the concerns that some Members have about using one minutes to communicate a party's daily message.[19] External factors such as "the rise of sound-bite politics" and the incentive of media coverage were also cited as encouraging partisan attacks and breaches of decorum during House floor debate.[20]

"CIVILITY" HEARINGS

The House Rules Committee's Subcommittee on Rules and Organization of the House held hearings on April 17, 1997, and May 1, 1997, to discuss issues raised in *Civility*. Dr. Kathleen Hall Jamieson, author of *Civility* and dean of the Annenberg School for Communication at the University of Pennsylvania, testified along with several other congressional experts. By coincidence, the April 17 hearing was interrupted by a House vote on the question of striking unparliamentary words spoken in a one-minute speech. Witnesses and subcommittee Members referred to this incident throughout the May 1 hearing.

Civility's recommendation that one-minute speeches be either eliminated or postponed until after legislative business was examined at both hearings. Two alternative recommendations were advanced in testimony. First, the idea of holding one-minute speeches only once a week was proposed.[21] Second, it was recommended that the Speaker allow one-minute speeches of a "factual nature" in the morning and those of a "political nature" after the completion of legislative business.[22]

Both hearings explored reinstating the so-called "Oxford-style" debates—another *Civility* recommendation—as a supplementary reform to changing House practices for one minutes.[23] In testimony on April 17, 1997, Dr. Jamieson recommended that "if we move or eliminate one-minute speeches, we conventionalize Oxford debates as an additional forum available. In Oxford debate, strong partisanship would be the rule, but in an environment in which the debate structure increases the likelihood that one arbitrates evidence and doesn't engage in personalities."[24] Suggestions for improving future Oxford-style debates, such as giving these debates a different name and allowing more Members to participate in them, were offered by witnesses at both hearings.

The House Rules Committee held hearings on the 1999 report on April 29, 1999.

End Notes

[1] Under House Rule XVII, clause 1(b)(1), a Member "shall be confined to the question under debate." Besides one-minute speeches, special orders (usually every day; five to 60 minutes in length) and morning hour debates (on Mondays and Tuesdays only; up to five minutes in length) provide other opportunities for non-legislative debate in the House.

[2] The *Journal* is the official record of the proceedings of the House.

[3] These precedents are published in several parliamentary reference publications. For more information, see CRS Report RL30787, *Parliamentary Reference Sources: House of Representatives*, by Richard S. Beth and Megan S. Lynch.

[4] U.S. Congress, House, *House Practice: A Guide to the Rules, Precedents and Procedures of the House*, 112th Cong., 1st sess. (Washington: GPO, 2011), "Consideration and Debate" chapter, sec. 50, p. 430-431.

[5] The 1984 announcement of these policies is provided in *Congressional Record*, daily edition, vol. 130, August 8, 1984, p. H8552. The Speaker's announced policies for the 113th Congress continued the application of these 1984 policies. See *Congressional Record*, daily edition, vol. 159, January 3, 2013, pp. H26.

[6] Ibid.

[7] Ibid.

[8] By contrast, special order and morning hour speeches must be reserved in advance through each party's leadership.

[9] Permission to *revise* gives Members the opportunity to make technical, grammatical, and typographical corrections only. Permission to *extend* authorizes the insertion of material such as a newspaper article or constituent letter during the one-minute speech.

[10] *House Practice*, "Consideration and Debate" chapter, sec. 50, p. 430.

[11] "Extensions of Remarks" is the section where Members of the House can insert "a speech that was not actually delivered on the floor" or "extraneous materials related to the subject under discussion," with the House's permission. There are three sections in the daily *Congressional Record*: (1) the proceedings of the House; (2) the proceedings of the Senate; and (3) the "Extensions of Remarks."

[12] Rep. Steve Chabot, "Morning 1-Minute Speeches Serve Important Function," *Congressional Record*, daily edition, vol. 143, March 5, 1997, p. H727.

[13] Rep. W.J. (Billy) Tauzin, remarks in the House, *Congressional Record*, daily edition, vol. 142, May 1, 1996, p. H 4375.

[14] Kathleen Hall Jamieson, *Civility in the House of Representatives* (Philadelphia: Annenberg Public Policy Center, 1997), 108 p. Kathleen Hall Jamieson, *Civility in the House of Representatives:* the 105th Congress (Philadelphia: Annenberg Public Policy Center, 1999), 18 p.

[15] The full text of this letter is reprinted in: U.S. Congress, House Committee on Rules, *Congressional Reform* hearings before the Committee on Rules and joint hearings before the Subcommittee on Legislative and Budget Process and Subcommittee on Rules and Organization of the House of the Committee on Rules, Building on Change: Preparing for the 105th Congress, 104th Cong., 2nd sess., July 17, 24 and September 5, 12, 1996 (Washington: GPO, 1996), p. 262.

[16] Ibid., p. 258

[17] Ibid., pp. 259-260.

[18] Jamieson, *Civility*, p. 54.

[19] Ibid.

[20] Ibid., p. 52.

[21] Testimony of Dr. Stephen Frantzich, chairman of the Department of Political Science, U.S. Naval Academy, May 1, 1997.

[22] Testimony of Donald Wolfensberger, guest scholar at the Woodrow Wilson International Center for Scholars, April 17, 1997.

[23] Three "Oxford-style" debates, two hours of structured debate with four participants from each party, were held on an experimental basis in the 103rd Congress.

[24] Testimony of Dr. Kathleen Hall Jamieson, April 17, 1997.

In: Federal Speeches: Policy and Practices   ISBN: 978-1-61761-755-3
Editor: Kathleen Weldon   © 2014 Nova Science Publishers, Inc.

Chapter 5

MORNING HOUR DEBATES: CURRENT HOUSE PRACTICES[*]

Judy Schneider

SUMMARY

On Mondays and Tuesdays, the House of Representatives meets earlier than the hour established for that day's session for a period called "morning hour debates" (also known as "morning hour speeches"). This period provides a rare opportunity for non-legislative debate in the House; remarks in the House are usually limited to pending legislative business. During morning hour debates, individual Members deliver speeches on topics of their choice for up to five minutes. The majority and minority leaders give the Speaker a list showing how each party's time for morning hour debates will be allocated among its Members. The chair follows this list in recognizing Members for morning hour debates. At the conclusion of morning hour debates, the House recesses until the starting time for that day's session. This report examines current House practices for morning hour debates and how these debates are used.

---

[*] This is an edited, reformatted and augmented version of Congressional Research Service Publication, No. RS20131, dated April 6, 2009.

BACKGROUND

Morning hour debates have been a part of House floor procedure only since the 103rd Congress.[1] They began on February 23, 1994, for a 90-day trial period under procedures outlined in a joint leadership unanimous consent agreement (formally, "a standing order of the House").[2] Morning hour debates were created, in part, to offset the new restrictions on special order speeches that took effect the same day. These restrictions, such as a ban on special orders after midnight and a four-hour limitation on longer special orders, scaled back opportunities for non-legislative debate available through special orders.[3]

The 1994 agreement establishing morning hour debates for a 90-day trial period was later extended to cover the remainder of the 103rd Congress. Morning hour debates continued in the 104th Congress under a slightly modified unanimous consent agreement. The modification concerned the length and starting time of morning hour debates on Tuesdays "after the first Tuesday in May" (see the "Days and Meeting Times" section for more information). An identical unanimous consent agreement (agreed to on January 6, 2009) governs morning hour speeches in the 111th Congress.[4]

GOVERNING AUTHORITIES

Morning hour debates are not provided for in the rules of the House. Instead, they are a *unanimous consent practice* of the chamber. The House gives unanimous consent to holding morning hour debates when it agrees to the joint leadership unanimous consent agreement governing these debates. In the 111th Congress, the chair refers to this agreement at the start of the morning hour debate period when he announces, "[p]ursuant to the order of the House of January 6, 2009, the Chair will now recognize ..." The unanimous consent agreement governs recognition for morning hour debates and establishes the days and meeting times for these debates (for more information, see later sections of this report).

During morning hour debates, Members must abide not only by the unanimous consent agreement but also by the rules of the House, the chamber's precedents, and the Speaker's announced policies. Relevant House rules include those governing debate, decorum, and the Speaker's power of recognition. House precedents discuss how the chamber has interpreted and applied its rules.[5] There is not an established body of precedents for morning hour debates because these debates are a relatively new feature of House floor procedure.

The term "Speaker's announced policies" refers to the Speaker's policies on certain aspects of House procedure such as decorum in debate, the conduct of electronic votes, and recognition for one-minute and special order speeches. While the Speaker's announced policies do not govern recognition for morning hour debates (the unanimous consent agreement governs recognition), they do regulate television coverage of morning hour debates. The Speaker's policies prohibit House-controlled television cameras from panning the chamber during the morning hour debate period. Instead, a caption (also called a "crawl") appears at the bottom of the television screen indicating that the House is conducting morning hour debates.[6]

DAYS AND MEETING TIMES

Morning hour debates are in order only on Mondays and Tuesdays. They take place infrequently on Mondays because the House is not always in session that day.

The starting time and length of morning hour debates are established by the joint leadership unanimous consent agreement. The House convenes for *Monday* morning hour debates 90 minutes earlier than the time established for that day's session. For example, if the House is scheduled to meet at noon, the morning hour debate period begins at 10:30 a.m. The Monday morning hour debate period can last up to one hour, with a maximum of 30 minutes of debate on each side. The full hour is rarely used. *Tuesday* morning hour speeches on or before May 18, 2009, take place in the same manner as Monday morning hour debates. The agreement provides, however, that *Tuesday* morning hour debates after May 18, 2009, begin 60 minutes before the chamber's meeting hour for a maximum duration of 50 minutes, with 25 minutes allocated to each side.

The different procedures for *Tuesday* morning debates after early May were first established in the joint leadership unanimous consent agreement of May 12, 1995.[7] These procedures, which are included in the agreement for the 111th Congress, are designed to accommodate the chamber's practice of convening earlier for legislative business after early May. In the 105th Congress, the procedures were only on those Tuesdays after early May when the House was scheduled to meet at 10:00 a.m.[8] On Tuesdays after early May when the chamber's appointed meeting hour was a later time (e.g., 12:00 noon), the Tuesday morning debates took place in the same manner as Monday morning hour debates.

When Monday and Tuesday morning hour debates are completed, the House recesses until the meeting hour established for that day's session. The daily prayer, the pledge of allegiance, and approval of the previous day's *Journal* take place when the House meets after this recess.

RECOGNITION PRACTICES

The joint leadership unanimous consent agreement requires that the majority and minority leaders give the Speaker a list showing how each party's time for morning hour debates will be allocated among its Members. The chair follows this list in recognizing Members for morning hour debates. A majority party Representative appointed as "Speaker *pro tempore*" often presides in the chair during morning hour debates. During each morning hour debate period, he alternates recognition between the majority and minority for both the *initial* morning hour speech (i.e., if a majority Member is recognized for the first speech on Monday, a minority Member is recognized for first speech on Tuesday) and *subsequent* ones. Individual Members must limit their morning hour debate speech to five minutes or less. Only the majority leader, minority leader, or the minority whip may deliver a morning hour debate speech longer than five minutes.

RESERVATION REQUIREMENTS

Members reserve time for morning hour debates through their party leadership: *Democratic* Representatives reserve time through the Office of the Minority Leader, and *Republican* Members do so through the Republican cloakroom or the party leadership desk on the House floor. Reservations can be made no earlier than one week before the speech date. While most Members reserve five minutes for their morning hour speech, some Representatives reserve as little as one minute.

VARIOUS USES OF MORNING HOUR DEBATES

Individual Members often use the morning hour debate period to deliver speeches on subjects unrelated to legislation before the House. They deliver eulogies and tributes to individuals and organizations from their congressional district. They also use the period to deliver speeches on broad policy issues and to present their views on local, national, and international events.

Because morning hour debates take place early in the day, they are sometimes used by individual Members and the party leadership to share information relevant to that day's session. For example, Members deliver morning hour speeches to explain a bill they are introducing that day and to invite cosponsors. The chairman of the Rules Committee has spoken during morning hour debates to announce an emergency meeting of the committee.[9] This use of morning hour debates to disseminate information among colleagues parallels how Members often employ one-minute speeches as a visual form of the "Dear Colleague" letter.

On occasion, Members of the same party use the morning hour debate period to deliver a series of speeches about the party's views on a particular bill or policy issue. For example, on February 11, 1997, four minority party Members delivered morning hour debate speeches on campaign finance reform.[10] This coordinated use of morning hour debates by party Members is similar to how the parties sometimes use "leadership special orders" (i.e., the first hour of longer special orders that is usually reserved for the party's leadership or a designee) to focus on a specific theme with participation from other party Members.

End Notes

[1] Under House Rules XVII, clause 1(b), a Member "shall be confined to the question under debate." Besides morning hour debates, one-minute speeches (usually at the start of every day) and special orders (5 to 60 minutes in length, usually at the end of every day) also provide opportunities for non-legislative debate in the House.

[2] The House consented to this agreement on February 11, 1994. *Congressional Record*, daily edition, vol. 140, February 11, 1994, p. H542.

[3] These new restrictions were announced by the Speaker on February 11, 1994. *Congressional Record*, daily edition, vol. 140, February 11, 1994, p. H542.

[4] *Congressional Record*, daily edition, January 6, 2009, p. H21.

[5] These precedents are published in several parliamentary reference publications. For more information, see CRS Report RL30787, *Parliamentary Reference Sources: House of Representatives*, by Richard S. Beth and Megan Suzanne Lynch.

[6] The Speaker first announced this policy on January 4, 1995. The policy was extended to cover the 111th Congress on January 6, 2009. See *Congressional Record*, daily edition, January 6, 2009, p. H21.

[7] *Congressional Record*, daily edition, vol. 141, May 12, 1995, p. H4901.

[8] For example, see *Congressional Record*, daily edition, vol. 143, July 29, 1997, pp. H5921-H5926. Morning hour debates began at 9:00 a.m. on this day when the meeting hour was set for 10:00 a.m.

[9] *Congressional Record*, daily edition, vol. 143, April 14, 1997, p. H1443.

[10] *Congressional Record*, daily edition, vol. 143, February 11, 1997, pp. H409-H411.

In: Federal Speeches: Policy and Practices ISBN: 978-1-61761-755-3
Editor: Kathleen Weldon   © 2014 Nova Science Publishers, Inc.

Chapter 6

THE SPEECH OR DEBATE CLAUSE: CONSTITUTIONAL BACKGROUND AND RECENT DEVELOPMENTS[*]

Alissa M. Dolan and Todd Garvey

SUMMARY

Members of Congress have immunity for their legislative acts under Article I, Section 6, clause 1, of the Constitution, which provides in part that "for any speech or debate in either House, [Senators and Representatives] shall not be questioned in any other place." Even if their actions are within the scope of the Speech or Debate Clause or some other legal immunity, Members of Congress remain accountable to the house of Congress in which they serve and to the electorate. In cases in which the Clause applies, the immunity is absolute and cannot be defeated by an allegation of an improper purpose or motivation. When applicable, the Clause provides both immunity from liability (in civil and criminal proceedings) and a complimentary evidentiary privilege.

Recently, two separate and previously unresolved issues arose with respect to the scope and application of the Speech or Debate Clause. The first case concerned claims of employment discrimination brought against Members' offices pursuant to the Congressional Accountability Act of

[*] This is an edited, reformatted and augmented version of a Congressional Research Service publication, CRS Report for Congress R42648, prepared for Members and Committees of Congress, from www.crs.gov, dated August 8, 2012.

1995. Both the Tenth Circuit Court of Appeals and the D.C. Circuit ruled that the Speech or Debate Clause does not automatically prevent such suits from proceeding. Additionally, an appeal to the Supreme Court was rejected because the Court ruled that it lacked a jurisdictional basis to decide the case.

These decisions, however, appear to leave unanswered significant questions about the use and introduction of evidence related to "legislative acts," which are protected by the Speech or Debate Clause. Such questions could ultimately frustrate the ability of potential plaintiffs to pursue their claims successfully.

In August 2007, the Court of Appeals for the District of Columbia Circuit (D.C. Circuit) issued its opinion in a case arising from the execution of a search warrant on the Rayburn House Office of Representative William J. Jefferson. The search was conducted as part of the FBI's investigation of Representative Jefferson to determine whether he was involved in criminal activity, including bribery and other felonies. Such an action by the executive branch appears to be unprecedented. It raised significant constitutional questions about potential intimidation of the legislative branch and threats to its independence, which the Clause is designed to protect.

Although Representative Jefferson lost his initial legal challenge, the appeals court subsequently held that the search violated the Speech or Debate Clause. The court ordered the district court to provide Representative Jefferson with copies of the seized materials and a chance to assert his privilege claims ex parte and in camera. Moreover, the appeals court ordered that the Department of Justice (DOJ) continue to refrain from reviewing any of the seized materials until the privilege claims were evaluated by the lower court.

In 2011, the Ninth Circuit Court of Appeals also weighed in on how to apply the Clause to executive branch criminal investigations of Members. In that case, Representative Richard Renzi was accused of agreeing to support legislation in exchange for a private land purchase agreement benefitting one of his creditors. He was indicted on numerous criminal counts, including extortion and fraud, which he challenged on Speech or Debate Clause grounds.

The appeals court determined that his challenged actions were not covered by the Clause. Additionally, the Ninth Circuit appeared to split with the D.C. Circuit analysis in Representative Jefferson's case on whether the Clause prevents the executive branch from ever viewing protected evidence.

This report examines the constitutional background of the Speech or Debate Clause and these recent developments in jurisprudence.

CONSTITUTIONAL BACKGROUND

The Constitution provides that "for any speech or debate in either House, [Senators and Representatives] shall not be questioned in any other place."[1] Commonly referred to as the Speech or Debate Clause, this language affords Members of Congress immunity from certain civil and criminal suits relating to their legislative acts.[2] In addition, the clause also provides a testimonial privilege[3] that extends not only to oral testimony about privileged matters[4] but to the production of privileged documents.[5]

Adopted at the Constitutional Convention without debate or opposition,[6] historically, the Speech or Debate Clause has been clearly understood to protect the "independence and integrity" of the legislature, allowing Members of Congress the freedom of speech, debate, and deliberation without fear of intimidation by the executive branch or the judiciary.[7] In explaining the purposes of the Speech or Debate Clause, the Supreme Court traced the ancestry of the Clause to the English Bill of Rights of 1689, which was "the culmination of a long struggle for parliamentary supremacy":

> Behind these simple phrases lies a history of conflict between the Commons and the Tudor and Stuart monarchs during which successive monarchs utilized the criminal and civil law to suppress and intimidate critical legislators. Since the Glorious Revolution in Britain, and throughout United States history, the privilege has been recognized as an important protection of the independence and integrity of the legislature.[8]

The Supreme Court has recognized that the Clause was not intended simply "for the personal or private benefit of Members of Congress, but to protect the integrity of the legislative process by insuring the independence of individual legislators."[9] The Court has also expressly noted that "the [C]lause serves the additional function of reinforcing the separation of powers so deliberately established by the Founders."[10] Moreover, the Court has "without exception ... read the Speech or Debate Clause broadly to effectuate its purposes."[11]

What Actions Are Protected by the Clause?

In its first decision interpreting the Clause, *Kilbourn v. Thompson*,[12] the Supreme Court read the Clause's protection expansively, applying it "to things generally done in a session of the House by one of its Members in relation to the business before it."[13] However, in *Gravel v. United States* and *United States v. Brewster*, two decisions issued on the same day in 1972, the Court adopted a more limited view of the Clause's protection. Not all actions taken by a Member in the course of his congressional duties are covered by the Speech or Debate Clause. As the Court explained,

> The heart of the Clause is speech or debate in either House. Insofar as the Clause is construed to reach other matters, they must be an *integral part of the deliberative and communicative processes* by which members participate in committee and House proceedings with respect to the consideration and passage or rejection of proposed legislation or with respect to other matters which the Constitution places within the jurisdiction of either House.[14]

Legislative Acts

Since the *Gravel* and *Brewster* rulings, the Clause has only protected a "legislative act," which is "an act generally done in Congress in relation to the business before it."[15] The Clause does not protect "political" activities, which include such activities as constituent services and issuing press releases, even if done as part of the Member's congressional duties. The *Brewster* Court explained that "[a]lthough these are entirely legitimate activities, they are political in nature rather than legislative" and, therefore, are not afforded Speech or Debate Clause protection.

This distinction between legislative acts and other legitimate, but non-legislative, acts can be seen in *Hutchinson v. Proxmire*.[16] In *Proxmire*, a Senator argued that the Speech or Debate Clause immunized him from liability for allegedly defamatory statements he made about a federal employee in his efforts to publicize wasteful government spending. The newsletters, press releases, and television interviews he gave to draw attention to the issue of government spending were not essential to the deliberation of the Senate and, therefore, received no Speech or Debate Clause protection. However, the same statements made in "a speech by Proxmire in the Senate would be wholly immune"[17] from defamation liability.

Criminal Acts

Additionally, the Clause does not protect criminal conduct that is not part of the "due functioning" of the legislative process.[18] A Member can still be prosecuted for criminal offenses such as bribery, since for example, accepting a bribe in exchange for voting a certain way is not "an integral part of the deliberative and communicative processes" by which Members participate in legislative activities.[19] However, the Clause's testimonial privilege will still prevent the introduction of evidence of true legislative acts or the motivation for such acts during such a prosecution.[20] As the *Gravel* court summarized, "While the ... clause recognizes speech, voting, and other legislative acts as exempt from liability that might otherwise attach, it does not privilege either Senator or aide to violate an otherwise valid criminal law in preparing for or implementing legislative acts."[21]

The distinction between covered legislative acts and unprotected criminal acts is demonstrated in *Gravel* and *Brewster*. In *Gravel*, the Court held that the Speech of Debate Clause prevented a grand jury from inquiring into the conduct or motives of a Senator or his aides[22] at a subcommittee meeting in which the Senator placed classified government documents, the Pentagon Papers, in the public record. However, the Court also held that the Clause did not prohibit the grand jury from probing how the Senator had obtained the Pentagon Papers or considering allegations that the Senator arranged for private publications of the classified materials. [23] The Court explained the distinction by stating, "While the ... clause recognizes speech, voting and other legislative acts as exempt from liability that might otherwise attach, it does not privilege either Senator or aide to violate an otherwise valid criminal law in preparing for or implementing legislative acts."[24]

Similarly, in *Brewster*, the Court determined that the Speech or Debate Clause did not provide immunity from prosecution for bribery, where a Member allegedly accepted payment in exchange for a promise to vote a specific way. The Court explained that the Clause has never been viewed "as protecting all conduct *relating* to the legislative process."[25] Because bribery was "not, by any conceivable interpretation, an act performed as part of or even incidental to the role of a legislator,"[26] it received no Speech or Debate Clause protection. Additionally, the Clause's testimonial privilege would not fatally harm the prosecution because "no inquiry into legislative acts or motivation for legislative acts is necessary for the Government to make out a prima facie case"[27] for bribery.

Overview of Protection

To summarize, the Supreme Court's interpretations and holdings in cases involving the Speech or Debate Clause indicate absolute protection for Members when speaking on the House or Senate floor,[28] introducing and voting on bills and resolutions,[29] preparing and submitting committee reports,[30] acting at committee meetings and hearings,[31] and conducting investigations and issuing subpoenas.[32]

Conversely, the Clause "does not prohibit inquiry into activities that are casually or incidentally related to legislative affairs" or a Member's congressional duties, "but not a part of the legislative process itself."[33] The Court has identified these acts to include speaking outside of Congress,[34] writing newsletters,[35] issuing press releases,[36] private book publishing,[37] distribution of official committee reports outside of the legislative sphere,[38] and constituent services.[39]

Who Can be Protected by the Clause?

The Speech or Debate Clause protection applies not only to Members, but also to their aides, who "are to be 'treated as one.'"[40] The Clause protects an aide's action when the Clause would have protected the same action if it was done by a Member. The Clause is interpreted as extending its protection to aides because the *Gravel* Court recognized

> that it is literally impossible, in view of the complexities of the modern legislative process, with Congress almost constantly in session and matters of legislative concern constantly proliferating, for Members of Congress to perform their legislative tasks without the help of aides and assistants; that the day-to-day work of such aides is so critical to the Members' performance that they must be treated as the latter's alter egos; and that if they are not so recognized, the central role of the Speech or Debate Clause—to prevent intimidation of legislators by the Executive and accountability before a possibly hostile judiciary will inevitably be diminished and frustrated.[41]

Furthermore, the Clause affords both an institutional and an individual privilege.[42] It is uncertain whether, at least in limited circumstances, the institution might be able to waive the privilege of individual Members.[43] The Court has assumed, without deciding, that an individual Member could waive the Clause's protection against criminal prosecution, but has held that such a waiver could "be found only after explicit and unequivocal renunciation of the protection."[44]

It has been held that the Clause may be asserted not only by a current Member but also by a former Member in an action implicating his conduct while in Congress[45] and by a Member's "aides insofar as the conduct of the latter would be a protected legislative act if performed by the Member himself."[46] The immunity applies regardless of whether the Member or aide is a party to the litigation or has merely been called to testify or give a deposition.[47]

RECENT CASES

Employment and Personnel Actions

For some time now, there has been an open question as to whether the Speech or Debate Clause protects a Member from liability in civil actions arising from office personnel disputes. In 1995, with little debate focused on the immunity issue, the House and Senate passed the Congressional Accountability Act (CAA),[48] which applies several civil rights, labor, and workplace safety and health laws to Congress.[49] Section 413 of the CAA, however, declares that the authorization to bring judicial proceedings under various provisions of the law does not constitute a waiver of the Speech or Debate privilege of any Member.[50]

Prior to the passage of the CAA, the United States Court of Appeals for the District of Columbia (D.C. Circuit) had held that the Speech or Debate Clause provided Members with immunity from personnel actions brought by at least some congressional employees. In *Browning v. Clerk, U.S. House of Representatives*,[51] it was alleged that the termination of the first African American Official Reporter employed by the House was the result of racial animus.[52] The court, in dismissing the claims, held that the Speech or Debate Clause protected Members from liability based on personnel actions they took if the impacted "employee's duties were directly related to the due functioning of the legislative process."[53]

However, two years later, the Supreme Court raised doubts as to whether Speech or Debate Clause immunity extended to employment actions. In *Forrester v. White*,[54] a case alleging sex discrimination, the Court held that a state court judge did not have judicial immunity for the firing of a probation officer. It concluded that the immunity did not extend to "administrative, legislative, or executive functions," regardless of how important the functions may be to the "very functioning of the court."[55] In other words, according to the Court, the employment decision in *Forrester* was administrative, not judicial; therefore, there was no entitlement to judicial immunity.[56] Subsequently, in *Gross v. Winter*,[57] the D.C. Circuit, applying *Forrester*, held that common-law legislative immunity did not immunize a D.C. Council Member from suit based on employment-related decisions.[58] However, the court in *Gross* declined to overturn the reasoning in *Browning*, preferring instead to distinguish the case on the grounds that it dealt with a common law privilege and not the Speech or Debate Clause.

In light of the passage of the CAA and these previous cases, both the Tenth Circuit Court of Appeals[59] and the D.C. Circuit[60] have weighed in on this issue, rejecting arguments that the Speech or Debate Clause protection requires automatic dismissal of employment-related civil cases.

Bastien v. Campbell

In 2002, the United States District Court for the District of Colorado heard the first case applying the Speech or Debate Clause to an employment discrimination allegation brought pursuant to the CAA.[61] The plaintiff, a former district office staffer for Senator Ben Nighthorse Campbell, alleged age discrimination and retaliation for discrimination complaints and sought relief under the CAA. The Senator's office moved to dismiss the claims, arguing that the Speech or Debate Clause immunized the office from the claims because the "[p]laintiff's duties of meeting with constituents, gathering information for the Senator, discussing constituent suggestions and then conveying them to the Senator, constitute actions that directly relate to the due functioning of the legislative process."[62] The district court found that the plaintiff's duties included "gathering and conveying to Senator Campbell himself, and to the Defendant, information critical to the Senator's legislative agenda."[63] As a result, the court dismissed the suit, holding that because the plaintiff's duties were directly related to the due functioning of the legislative process, the Speech or Debate Clause immunity applied.[64]

The Court of Appeals for the Tenth Circuit, however, reversed the lower court's decision, distinguishing between "legislative" acts that are entitled to Speech or Debate immunity and non-legislative acts, which are not.[65] Senator Campbell argued that the plaintiff's job function constituted a legislative act because the information received from constituents could affect his drafting and support of legislation and his votes. The court disagreed, classifying such functions as "informal information gathering" that is distinct from the type of information gathering performed by legislative committees, which is covered by the Speech or Debate Clause.[66] Extending the Clause's protection to other forms of information gathering by individual Members would exceed the Supreme Court's interpretation of the Clause's scope.[67] Therefore, the Clause's protection did not apply because the allegedly discriminatory actions by the Senator were not legislative acts. Additionally, the Clause's testimonial privilege would not hamper this civil action because the "[p]laintiff's discrimination claim does not require proof of any legislative act by Senator Campbell or his staff."[68]

The court did note that even if the Senator's actions were protected, the Senator's office could still be liable for personnel decisions because an office's actions fall outside the scope of the Clause's immunity.[69] Moreover, the court specifically refused to adopt the D.C. Circuit's reasoning in *Browning v. Clerk*, noting that, in its opinion, *Browning* extended further than the Supreme Court's cases involving the Speech or Debate Clause. However, the court did note that even if it had adopted the *Browning* standard, this employee's case would be entitled to proceed because the duties performed were not central to the legislative process and, therefore, not entitled to the Speech or Debate Clause's protection.[70]

Fields v. Office of Eddie Bernice Johnson and Hanson v. Office of Senator Dayton

The Tenth Circuit's decision in *Bastien* created a conflict between the circuits that led the D.C. Circuit to consolidate two pending cases and hear them en banc.[71] The two cases involved, respectively, the House office of the Honorable Eddie Bernice Johnson and the office of Senator Mark Dayton. The D.C. Circuit examined whether employment suits brought under the CAA must be dismissed because of the Speech or Debate Clause and whether *Browning v. Clerk of U.S House of Representatives* should remain the law of the circuit.[72] With 8 of the 10 members of the D.C. Circuit participating, the court unanimously decided that the Speech or Debate Clause does not require the dismissal of suits brought under the CAA.[73] The court also unanimously held that the *Browning* framework was no longer consistent with Supreme Court precedent and should be abandoned.[74]

Despite this agreement that automatic dismissal was unwarranted, the court splintered when determining the appropriate scope of Speech or Debate Clause applicability after the plaintiff has established a prima facie case of discrimination. On the one hand, Judge Randolph's plurality opinion focused on the interaction between the judicially created, burden-shifting framework used in employment discrimination cases and the Clause's potential protections.[75] Under the framework, a plaintiff proves a prima facie case of discrimination, then the employer rebuts by producing evidence that the conduct was nondiscriminatory, and, finally, the plaintiff tries to demonstrate that the employer's explanation is pretextual.[76] If the employer's nondiscriminatory reason for taking the adverse employment action is motivated by a legislative act, the Speech or Debate Clause protection may prevent a plaintiff from being able to challenge the Member's assertion,[77] since Members remain protected from "inquiry into legislative acts or the motivation for actual performance of legislative acts."[78]

Judge Randolph attempts to provide some guidelines for invoking the Clause's protection[79] and emphasizes that the Clause's application must be determined on a case-by-case basis.[80]

On the other hand, Judge Janice Rodgers Brown, writing for three members of the court, noted that the CAA creates a "legal fiction" by holding the Member's "employing office" liable for employment discrimination claims, not the Member or his aides individually.[81] She concluded that the "employing office," as an "organizational division within Congress," is not entitled to Speech or Debate Clause protection.[82] Judge Brown did recognize that the Clause's evidentiary privilege would protect the Member from disclosure or discussion of his legislative acts if he was personally implicated.[83]

Judge Brown appears to suggest a narrower reading of the Speech or Debate Clause than offered by Judge Randolph's plurality opinion. According to Judge Brown's opinion, as long as a Member or potentially protected aide is not directly providing evidence or giving testimony, the Speech or Debate Clause is not implicated; therefore, plaintiffs can potentially pursue more claims under this interpretation.[84] However, if the suit requires such evidence or testimony, even Judge Brown's interpretation would require a district court to address assertions of Speech or Debate immunity on a case-by-case basis.[85]

Senator Dayton's office filed a petition for writ of certiorari to the Supreme Court, along with a statement of jurisdiction asserting that the CAA afforded his office an appeal by right to the Court.[86] The Court set oral arguments for April 24, 2007, to address whether the office was entitled to a direct appeal to the Supreme Court and whether the case was now moot because Senator Dayton's term of office had expired.[87] The Court issued its decision on May 21, 2007, unanimously holding that it lacked jurisdiction to reach the merits of the case.[88] Senator Dayton based his request for review on Section 412 of the CAA, which states that "[a]n appeal may be taken directly to the Supreme Court of the United States from any interlocutory or final judgment, decree, or order of a court *upon the constitutionality of any provision of this chapter.*"[89] According to the Court, this section cannot serve as the basis for jurisdiction because the D.C. Circuit's "determination that jurisdiction attaches despite a claim of Speech or Debate Clause immunity is best read as a ruling on the scope of the Act, not its constitutionality."[90] The Court also concluded that there was no basis for exercising its discretionary certiorari jurisdiction as the D.C. Circuit's decision did not conflict with any other circuit with respect to the application of the Speech or Debate Clause in suits challenging personnel actions taken by Members of Congress.[91] Senator Dayton's office went back to the district court after its Speech or Debate Clause argument was rejected and the court denied its motion to dismiss arguing that the claim was moot.[92] News reports indicate that Senator Dayton settled the claim in February 2009.[93] Representative Johnson's office ultimately prevailed on the merits of the employee's discrimination claims in district court[94] and the subsequent appeal was voluntarily dismissed in 2008.[95]

Executive Branch Criminal Investigations of Members

In recent years, both the D.C. Circuit and the Ninth Circuit have issued opinions addressing the application of the Speech or Debate Clause privilege to executive branch criminal investigations of Members. In both cases, *United States v. Rayburn House Office Building* and *United States v. Renzi*, the underlying criminal investigation concerned bribery, a non-legislative act that was not covered by the Clause. However, the appeals courts had to assess how the Clause's privilege impacted the executive branch's effort to gather evidence throughout its investigations. In part, the courts addressed whether the Clause only prohibited the executive branch from introducing privileged documents into evidence during a court proceeding or whether it also prohibited the executive branch from ever viewing the documents at all. On this last point, the two circuits appear to split. The D.C. Circuit adopted a more expansive interpretation of the privilege, stating that it prevents the executive from viewing privileged documents at any stage. However, the Ninth Circuit interpretation is narrower, determining that the Clause only provided the Member with a non-use privilege at trial.

Searches and Seizures of Congressional Offices: United States v. Rayburn House Office Building

In March 2005, the FBI began an investigation of Representative William J. Jefferson to determine whether he and other persons had engaged in bribery and/or wire fraud.[96] The investigation centered on allegations that the Representative used his position to promote the sale of telecommunications equipment and services by a domestic firm to several African nations in return for stocks and cash and that he planned to bribe high-ranking Nigerian officials, amongst others, to obtain the necessary approval for the firm's ventures. On May 20, 2006, DOJ and FBI agents executed a valid search warrant at Representative Jefferson's congressional offices in the Rayburn Building.[97] The search lasted approximately 18 hours and resulted in the seizure of two boxes of paper records and electronic copies of the contents of every computer hard drive in the Representative's office. The General Counsel of the House of Representatives and Representative Jefferson's private counsel sought entry to the offices to oversee the search but were prohibited from doing so by the agents.[98]

The warrant's supporting affidavit contained special procedures to guide and confine the search process, recognizing the uniquely sensitive nature of searching a congressional office.[99] A search team of special agents from the FBI who had no role in the investigation (non-case agents) would examine every paper document in the office and determine which documents were responsive to the list of documents being sought. The non-case agents were forbidden from revealing any nonresponsive or politically sensitive information they came across during the search. Responsive documents were then transferred to a "filter team," consisting of two non-prosecution team DOJ attorneys and a non-case FBI agent, who reviewed the documents to determine responsiveness and whether the Speech or Debate Clause protection could apply. Responsive documents not covered by the Speech or Debate Clause were to be transferred to the prosecution team, which had to provide copies to Representative Jefferson's counsel. Papers potentially covered by the Clause were to be recorded in a log to be given, along with copies of the papers, to counsel. According to the warrant, the potentially privileged papers were not to be supplied to the prosecution team until a court so ordered.

Furthermore, a special FBI forensics team would download all electronic files from the office computers and transfer them to an FBI facility, where a search using court-approved search terms would be conducted. Responsive data were to be turned over to the filter team. Responsive, potentially privileged computer documents were to be recorded in a log to be given to counsel, along with copies of the documents. The filter team would then request the court to review the potentially privileged records.[100]

Speech or Debate Clause Legal Arguments

The purpose of the Speech or Debate Clause protection is to insulate Members and the legislature from intimidation by the executive or the judiciary and reinforce the separation of powers among the co-equal branches.

Allowing the FBI, an executive branch entity, to make the initial legal and constitutional determinations of which documents seized from a Member's congressional office are protected by the Clause arguably endangers Congress's autonomy and exposes it to future intimidation by the executive. Therefore, conducting a search of a congressional office following the procedures discussed above could arguably undermine the very purpose of the Speech or Debate Clause, which might not be mitigated even if the documents are later ruled inadmissible in court since the executive has already studied the full contents of the Member's office.

A former Deputy Attorney General in the Reagan Administration testified before the House Judiciary Committee and summarized these concerns:

> The Clause is offended the moment the F.B.I. peruses a constitutionally protected legislative document. Even if the document is not seized, memory of its political contents remains in the Executive Branch for use in thwarting congressional opposition or leaking embarrassing political information... . The knowledge by a Member that the F.B.I. can make an unannounced raid on his legislative office to read and rummage through every document or email is bound to discourage Congress from the muscular check against the Executive that the Speech or Debate Clause was calculated to foster.[101]

Representative Jefferson raised these Speech or Debate Clause arguments when he sought to have the search declared unconstitutional and the seized materials returned to his possession.[102] In addition to raising many of the arguments discussed above, Representative Jefferson argued, inter alia, that execution of the search warrant "guaranteed that the executive would be in possession of material that relates to the Member's legislative duties."[103] The motion asserted that those actions, coupled with the exclusion of Representative Jefferson's counsel and the House General Counsel from even viewing the search process, violated his Speech or Debate Clause privilege.[104]

The DOJ argued in its reply brief that because it was only interested in obtaining non-legislative materials, the use of a filter team provided sufficient protection of the privilege under the Speech or Debate Clause.[105] The DOJ appeared to be arguing that the Clause's language "shall not be questioned at any other place" merely protects Members from having information relating to legislative acts used against them in a criminal proceeding.[106] The DOJ's filing suggested that the past practice of using subpoenas to obtain documents and allowing the House General Counsel's Office initially to review and assess the privilege was simply a matter of "comity."[107] The DOJ also argued that

Representative Jefferson's position "would effectively extend Speech or Debate immunity to clearly unprivileged materials by making it impossible to execute a search warrant in any place containing even one privileged document."[108]

The DOJ's argument seemed to emphasize that the actual prosecution team never had access to any privileged information. Therefore, it argued, the Speech or Debate Clause was not violated.[109] Under this view, the Clause provides nothing more than an evidentiary privilege to be asserted prior to trial, which Representative Jefferson could still raise like a routine motion to exclude improperly seized evidence. To support this argument, the DOJ compared this search to other Member prosecutions where the DOJ made privilege determinations for documents it received pursuant to a subpoena.[110]

District Court Proceedings

The United States District Court for the District of Columbia rejected Representative Jefferson's arguments and upheld the search and seizure of materials from his Rayburn House Office as constitutional.[111] The court adopted an arguably narrow interpretation of the Clause, stating that a broader interpretation "would require a Member of Congress to be given advance notice of any search of his property, including property outside his congressional office ... and further that he be allowed to remove any material that he deemed to be covered by the legislative privilege prior to the search."[112] It also held that the Clause's testimonial privilege did not apply under the circumstances presented because unlike providing responses to a subpoena, having property searched pursuant to a search warrant is not a testimonial act.[113] In the court's view, the Speech or Debate Clause merely protects Members from having to "answer questions as to [their] legislative activities"; it "does not prohibit the disclosure of legislative material."[114]

The court compared the Speech or Debate Clause privilege to other common law privileged in upholding the filtering procedure employed by the FBI during the search. It rejected the notion that the Clause functionally required advanced notice of a search that might uncover privileged documents, since no other privilege mandated this notice.[115] Since Representative Jefferson remained free to assert the privilege at a later point in potential criminal proceedings against him, the search did not violate the Speech or Debate Clause.

After having his request for a stay pending appeal denied by the district court, Representative Jefferson filed notice of appeal to the U.S. Court of Appeals for the District of Columbia Circuit, seeking a stay of the lower court's order and any DOJ review of the seized documents.[116] A three-judge panel of the appeals court issued a two-page order remanding the case back to the district court for further fact finding with respect to claims of legislative privilege and detailing the procedures under which the court is to perform its duties.[117]

Court of Appeals Proceedings

Following the remand for further fact-finding, the court of appeals heard oral argument on Representative Jefferson's appeal on May 15, 2007, and issued its decision on August 3, 2007.[118] It concluded that the "compelled disclosure of privileged material to the Executive during execution of the search warrant ... violated the Speech or Debate Clause and that the Congressman is entitled to the return of documents that the court determines to be privileged under the Clause."[119] In reaching its conclusion, the court affirmed its holding in *Brown & Williamson Tobacco Corporation v. Williams*,[120] emphasizing that a critical component of the Speech or Debate Clause is the prevention of intrusions into the legislative process, and that the compelled disclosure of legislative materials is such a disruption, regardless of the proposed use of the material.[121]

Applying these principles to the search of Representative Jefferson's office, the court stated that

> this compelled disclosure clearly tends to disrupt the legislative process: exchanges between a Member of Congress and the Member's staff or among Members of Congress on legislative matters may legitimately involve frank or embarrassing statements; the possibility of compelled disclosure may therefore chill the exchange of views with respect to legislative activity. This chill runs counter to the Clause's purpose of protecting against disruption of the legislative process.[122]

The court carefully distinguished between the lawfulness of searching a congressional office pursuant to a search warrant—which the court held was clearly permissible—and the lawfulness of the way the search was executed considering the Member's potential Speech or Debate Clause protection.[123] Thus, it concluded that the Clause was violated because the executive's search procedures "denied the Congressman any opportunity to identify and assert the privilege with respect to legislative materials before their compelled disclosure to Executive agents."[124] The court declined, however, to expressly delineate acceptable procedures that could avoid this violation in future searches of congressional offices, noting only that there appears to be "no reason why the

Congressman's privilege under the Speech or Debate Clause cannot be asserted at the outset of a search in a manner that also protects the interests of the Executive in law enforcement."[125] Moreover, the court observed that the precise contours of those accommodations are a matter best left to negotiations between the political branches.[126]

Additionally, the court declined to grant Representative Jefferson's requested relief, a return of all of the seized documents. Instead, the court determined that its previous Remand Order "affords the Congressman an opportunity to assert the privilege prior to disclosure of privileged materials to the Executive" for electronic files.[127] With respect to the paper documents, the court concluded that, while the Clause's testimonial privilege prevents compelled disclosure of privileged documents, it does not prohibit "inquiry into illegal conduct simply because it has some nexus to legislative functions."[128] Therefore, according to the court, returning all of the seized documents would be an inappropriate remedy for a violation of the Speech or Debate Clause. Instead, Representative Jefferson was entitled only to a return of legislative documents covered by the Speech or Debate Clause. Non-privileged materials—which may yet be subject to future challenges as the criminal trial proceeds—did not have to be returned at that time.[129] Furthermore, the court ordered that "the FBI agents who executed the search warrant shall continue to be barred from disclosing the contents of any privileged or politically sensitive and non-responsive items, and they shall not be involved in the pending prosecution or other charges arising from the investigation."[130]

Representative Jefferson's specific privilege claims, based on his review of the documents pursuant to the court of appeals' remand order, were evaluated by the district court. The documents for which Representative Jefferson did not assert privilege were turned over to the DOJ for review. Ultimately, Representative Jefferson was convicted on 11 of the 16 bribery and fraud charges brought against him and received a 13-year prison sentence.[131] Ten of these 11 convictions were upheld by the Fourth Circuit Court of Appeals in March 2012.[132]

United States v. Renzi

In 2009, Former Representative Richard Renzi was indicted on 48 criminal counts including extortion, money laundering, wire fraud, insurance fraud, and conspiracy related to alleged *quid pro quo* deals he orchestrated while representing Arizona's first district in the House of Representatives.[133] Representative Renzi was accused of making deals with Resolution Copper Mining (RCC) and an investment group led by Philip Aries (Aries), in which the companies agreed to buy property owned by James Sandlin, his former business partner. In exchange, he promised to introduce a land exchange bill, which would propose swapping the Sandlin property for federally owned land for which the companies wished to attain ownership of surface rights, and steer it through the House Natural Resources Committee.[134] Mr. Sandlin owed Representative Renzi $700,000 and the purchase of his property would enable him to pay the debt back to Representative Renzi.[135]

During the course of the district court proceedings, Representative Renzi argued that the Speech or Debate Clause entitled him to (1) absolute immunity from prosecution because his negotiations with RCC and Aries were "legislative acts"; (2) dismissal of his indictment because privileged evidence was presented to the grand jury; and (3) a hearing to determine if the government used evidence protected by the Clause to obtain non-protected evidence.[136] The district court ruled against Representative Renzi on all three requests and he filed an interlocutory appeal with the Court of Appeals for the Ninth Circuit.

The appeals court affirmed the district court's orders, holding that Representative Renzi's interactions and negotiations with RCC and Aries were not legislative acts, and therefore, were not protected by the Clause.[137] In coming to this conclusion, the appeals court emphasized that no court has ever "indicated that 'everything that related to the office of a Member was shielded by the Clause.'"[138] Additionally, the court noted that the Supreme Court has distinguished between completed legislative acts, which are covered by the clause, and promises to perform future legislative acts, which are not covered.[139] As the *Brewster* Court previously held, pre-legislative negotiations with private parties or constituents are not considered to be legislative acts because the Clause's text and history do not support such a broad reading of the privilege.[140] Furthermore, Representative Renzi's specific acts, his negotiations with RCC and Aries, cannot fall under the Clause's protection because extortion, like the bribery claims at issue in *Brewster*, has no part in the legislative process and is not performed as a part of a Member's role as legislator.[141]

Next, the Court addressed Representative Renzi's argument that his indictment should be dismissed because the grand jury was presented evidence of protected legislative acts. While generally a court will not inquire into the evidence used to support a grand jury indictment if the indictment is valid on its face, the grand jury is not permitted to violate a valid privilege, like the Speech or Debate Clause privilege. Therefore, other circuits have gone "behind the face of the indictment" when a violation of the Clause is alleged at the grand jury stage. In this case, the appeals court adopted the Eleventh Circuit test, concluding that it should look behind the face of the indictment and only dismiss it if protected "'evidence [presented to the grand jury] cause[d] the jury to indict.'"[142] The court noted that using this test protects the privilege without allowing Members to avoid prosecution for acts that are not protected by the Clause.[143] The appeals court found that several documents discussed actual legislative acts and should not have been presented to the grand jury. However, the court refused to dismiss the indictment because the protected evidence did not cause the jury to indict. Rather, the indictment relied on evidence of Representative Renzi's interactions with RCC and Aries, negotiations that the court previously concluded were not legislative acts and therefore were not protected.

The appeals court then addressed Representative Renzi's request for a hearing to determine if the government's non-protected evidence was derived from protected evidence, which he argued could not be used in the proceeding. In addressing this request, the court had to evaluate whether the Speech or Debate Clause privilege is a privilege of non-disclosure, as Representative Renzi maintained, or non-use, meaning the Clause only prevents protected evidence from being introduced in a court proceeding. The court rejected Representative Renzi's argument that the Clause confers a non-disclosure privilege, emphasizing that the Supreme Court has never held that the Clause prevents the use of derivative evidence or "precludes the Government from reviewing documentary evidence referencing 'legislative acts' even as part of an investigation into unprotected activity."[144]

This part of the decision puts the Ninth Circuit at odds with the D.C. Circuit decision in *United States v. Rayburn House Office Building*, discussed above, which concluded that the Clause prohibits any executive branch exposure to evidence of legislative acts.[145] The appeals court described the holding in *Rayburn* as founded on reasoning unique to the D.C. Circuit that has not been adopted by the Supreme Court. The court rejected the D.C. Circuit's interpretation that the "'distraction' of Members and their staffs from legislative tasks is a principal concern of the Clause" and, thus, distraction alone can trigger the Clause's protection.[146] Rather, the court stated that the risk of legislative distraction can only prompt the Clause's protection when the underlying investigation being conducted concerns a privileged legislative act. As the court explained, "[w]hen the Clause bars the underlying action, any investigation and litigation serve only as wasted exercises that *unnecessarily distract Members from their legislative tasks.*"[147] In its view, this is the type of distraction that the Clause is intended to prevent.

However, when the underlying action is not covered by the Clause, such as the investigations of alleged extortion and fraud in this case and *Rayburn*, other legitimate interests, like the ability of the executive branch to prosecute non-protected activities, outweigh concerns about legislative distraction.[148] The court relied upon the Supreme Court's holding in *United States v. Helstoski*,[149] a 1979 case prosecuting a Member for bribery, as support for its disagreement with the decision in *Rayburn*. In *Helstoski*, the Court held that the government could introduce into evidence documents discussing legislative acts, which it had obtained through compelled disclosure from the defendant Member, as long as the documents were redacted to exclude any references to legislative acts.[150] The appeals court stated that this outcome was irreconcilable with Representative Renzi's argument and the *Rayburn* holding. The Clause must be interpreted as providing a non-use privilege, not a non-disclosure privilege, "because the Executive would be hard pressed to redact a document it was constitutionally precluded from obtaining or reviewing...."[151]

The court also criticized the *Rayburn* decision for ignoring the fact that "the Speech or Debate Clause is a creature born of separation of powers concerns," and thus should apply equally to both the executive and the judiciary.[152] It reasoned that if the Clause provided a non-disclosure privilege, then disclosures of privileged documents to the executive branch and the judiciary would constitute independent violations.[153] Even though the *Rayburn* court adopted a nondisclosure interpretation and ruled that disclosures to the executive branch constituted violations of the Clause, it did not recognize that disclosures to the judiciary could also be violations.[154] Instead, it put the judiciary in charge of viewing and evaluating all of the allegedly privileged evidence.[155] The appeals court in *Renzi* used this internal inconsistency to reinforce its view that a non-disclosure interpretation of the clause was implausible and incorrect.[156]

Representative Renzi filed a petition for a writ of certiorari to the Supreme Court following the appeals court decision. His petition was denied in January 2012.[157] The criminal prosecution is still pending in the district court.

End Notes

[1] U.S. CONST. art. I, § 6, cl. 1.

[2] See e.g., United States v. Helstoski, 442 U.S. 477 (1979) (excluding evidence of legislative action in a criminal prosecution of a Member of the House of Representatives); Eastland v. United States Servicemen's Fund, 421 U.S. 491 (1975) (dismissing civil suit to enjoin a Senate Committee investigation) [hereinafter Eastland]; Dombrowski v. Eastland, 387 U.S. 82, 85 (1967) (dismissing a civil conspiracy claim against members of a Senate committee); United States v. Johnson, 383 U.S. 169 (1966) (reversing criminal conspiracy conviction based on Speech or Debate Clause immunity).

[3] See generally, Gravel v. United States, 408 U.S. 606 (1972).

[4] Id. at 615-16; see also Dennis v. Sparks, 449 U.S. 24, 30 (1980) (stating "we have held that Members of Congress need not respond to questions about their legislative acts"); Miller v. Transamerica Press, Inc., 709 F.2d 524, 528-29 (9th Cir. 1983) (denying a motion to compel testimony from a former Member of Congress).

[5] See, e.g., Maddox v. Williams, 855 F. Supp. 406, 413 (D.D.C. 1994) (stating that "the Speech or Debate Clause stands as an insuperable obstacle to [a party's] attempt to acquire by compulsion documents or copies of documents in the possession of the Congress") aff'd sub nom. Brown & Williamson Tobacco Corp. v. Williams, 62 F.3d 408 (D.C. Cir. 1995); see also Minpeco, S.A. v. Conticommodity Services, 844 F.2d 856, 859-61 (D.C. Cir. 1988) (applying a broad reading of the Clause to protect the "integrity of the legislative process itself"); Hearst v. Black, 87 F.2d 68, 71-2 (D.C. Cir. 1936) (stating that "[i]f a court could say to the Congress that it could use or could not use information in its possession, the independence of the Legislature would be destroyed and the constitutional separation of the powers of government invaded").

[6] See Powell v. McCormack, 395 U.S. 486, 502 (1969) (citing 5 DEBATES ON THE FEDERAL CONSTITUTION 406 (J. Elliot, ed. 1876); 2 RECORDS OF THE FEDERAL CONVENTION OF 1787, 246 (M. Farrand, rev. ed. 1966)).

[7] Johnson, 383 U.S. at 181.

[8] Id. at 178 (internal citations omitted); see also Tenney v. Brandhove, 341 U.S. 367, 372 (1951) (stating that:

The privilege of legislators to be free from arrest or civil process for what they do or say in legislative proceedings has taproots in the Parliamentary struggles of the Sixteenth and Seventeenth Centuries. As Parliament achieved increasing independence from the Crown, its statement of the privilege grew stronger. In 1523, Sir Thomas More could make only a tentative claim. ... In 1668, after a long and bitter struggle, Parliament finally laid the ghost of Charles I, who had prosecuted Sir John Elliot and others for "seditious" speeches in Parliament) (internal citations omitted).

[9] United States v. Brewster, 408 U.S. 501, 507 (1972); see also Kilbourn v. Thompson, 103 U.S. 168, 203 (1881).

[10] Johnson, 383 U.S. at 181.

[11] Eastland, 421 U.S. at 502.

[12] 103 U.S. 168 (1881).

[13] Id. at 204. The quoted language has been understood as extending immunity to "all 'things generally done'" in a congressional session by a Member in regard to pending business. Tribe, American Constitutional Law, vol. 1, at p. 1015 (3d ed. 2000) (emphasis added). For a similar interpretation of the quoted language, see Brewster, 408 U.S. at 509. The Kilbourn Court, 103 U.S. at 203-04, in rejecting a "narrow view of the constitutional provision" that would have limited it "to words spoken in debate," relied on the interpretation of a comparable clause in the Massachusetts Constitution in Coffin v. Coffin, 4 Mass. 1 (1808).

[14] Gravel, 408 U.S. at 625 (emphasis added).

[15] Brewster, 408 U.S. at 512.

[16] 443 U.S. 111.

[17] Id. at 130.

[18] Id. at 516; Gravel, 408 U.S. at 626 ("[The Clause] does not privilege either Senator or aide to violate an otherwise valid criminal law in preparing for or implementing legislative acts.").

[19] Gravel, 408 U.S. at 625; see Brewster, 408 U.S. at 525-26 ("Taking a bribe is, obviously, no part of the legislative process or function; it is not a legislative act. It is not, by any conceivable interpretation, an act performed as a part of or even incidental to the role of a legislator. It is not an 'act resulting from the nature, and in the execution, of the office.' Nor is it a 'thing said or done by him, as a representative, in the exercise of the functions of that office ... '" (internal citations omitted)).

[20] Brewster, 408 U.S. at 512. The prima facie case for bribery can be satisfied by showing that Member agreed to accept money in exchange for a promise to act a certain way. Since the prima facie case does not require a showing that the Member fulfilled that promise, the Speech or Debate Clause testimonial privilege is unlikely to burden such a prosecution. See id. at 525-26.

[21] Gravel, 408 U.S. at 626.

[22] See infra section "Who Can be Protected by the Clause?"

[23] Gravel, 408 U.S. at 609, 622-29.

[24] Id. at 626.

[25] Brewster, 408 U.S. at 515 (emphasis original).

[26] Id. at 526.

[27] Id. at 525.

[28] Johnson, 383 U.S. at 184-85; Gravel, 408 U.S. at 616; see also Cochran v. Couzens, 42 F.2d 783 (D.C. Cir. 1929), cert. denied, 282 U.S. 874 (1930).

[29] Powell, 395 U.S. at 505 (stating that "[t]he purpose of the protection afforded legislators is ... to insure that legislators are not distracted from or hindered in the performance of their legislative tasks by being called into court to defend their actions); Kilbourn, 103 U.S. at 204 (stating that "[t]he reason of the rule is as forcible in its application to written reports presented in that body by its committees, to resolutions offered, ... and to the act of voting, ... "); see also Fletcher v. Peck, 10 U.S. (6 Cranch) 87, 130 (1810) (declining to examine the motives of state legislators who were allegedly bribed for their votes).

[30] Doe v. McMillan, 412 U.S. 306, 311 (1973); Kilbourn, 103 U.S. at 204.

[31] See McMillan, 412 U.S. at 311; see also Gravel, 408 U.S. at 628-29. In addition, some lower federal courts have also held that the Clause bars the use of evidence of a Member's committee membership. Compare United States v. Swindall, 971 F.2d 1531 (11th Cir. 1991), rehearing denied, 980 F.2d 1449 (11th Cir. 1992) with United States v. McDade, 28 F.3d 283 (3d Cir. 1994), cert. denied, 514 U.S. 1003 (1995).

[32] See Eastland, 421 U.S. at 507; see also Tenney, 341 U.S. at 377 (refusing to examine motives of state legislator in summoning witness to hearing).

[33] Brewster, 408 U.S. at 528.

[34] Id. at 512.

[35] Id.

[36] Proxmire, 443 U.S. 111.

[37] Gravel, 408 U.S. at 625-26.

[38] McMillan, 412 U.S. at 315-16.

[39] Brewster, 408 U.S. at 512 (including "the making of appointments with Government agencies [and] assistance in securing Government contracts").

[40] Gravel, 408 U.S. at 616 (quoting United States v. Doe, 455 F.2d 753, 761 (1972).

[41] Id. at 616-17 (internal citations omitted).

[42] In re Grand Jury Investigation, 587 F.2d 589 (3d Cir. 1978). See also Helstoski, 442 U.S. at 492-93.

[43] In several cases, the Court specifically has declined to rule on the issue of waiver. See, e.g., Helstoski, 442 U.S. at 490; Brewster, 408 U.S. at 529 n.18; Johnson, 383 U.S. at 185.

[44] Id. at 490-91.

[45] See Brewster, 408 U.S. at 502.

[46] Gravel, 408 U.S. at 618.

[47] Miller v. Transamerican Press, 709 F.2d 524, 529 (9th Cir. 1983); Tavoulareas v. Piro, 93 F.R.D. 11, 18-19 (D.D.C. 1981).

[48] Congressional Accountability Act, P.L. 104-1, 109 Stat. 3 (1995).

[49] The CAA covers the following laws: Fair Labor Standards Act of 1938, Title VII of the Civil Rights Act of 1964, Americans with Disabilities Act of 1990, Age Discrimination in Employment Act of 1967, Family and Medical Leave Act of 1993, Occupational Safety and Health Act of 1970, Chapter 71 of Title 5 of the U.S. Code, Employee Polygraph Protection Act of 1988, Worker Adjustment and Retraining Notification Act, Rehabilitation Act of 1973, and Chapter 43 of Title 38 of the U.S. Code.

[50] Codified at 2 U.S.C. § 1413.

[51] 789 F.2d 923 (D.C. Cir. 1986), cert. denied, 479 U.S. 996 (1986).

[52] Id. at 924.

[53] Id. at 929.

[54] 484 U.S. 219 (1988).

[55] Id. at 227-28.

[56] Id. at 229-30.

[57] 876 F.2d 165 (D.C. Cir. 1989).

[58] Id. at 172 (stating that "the functions judges and legislators exercise in making personnel decisions affecting such employees are administrative, not judicial or legislative").

[59] Bastien v. Office of Senator Ben Nighthorse Campbell, 209 F. Supp. 2d 1095 (D. Colo. 2002) (holding that Speech or Debate immunity did apply to employment actions) [hereinafter Bastien I], rev'd, Bastien v. Office of Senator Ben Nighthorse Campbell, 390 F.3d 1301 (10th Cir. 2004) [hereinafter Bastien II].

[60] Fields v. Office of Eddie Bernice Johnson, 459 F.3d 1 (D.C. Cir. 2006).

[61] Bastien I, 209 F. Supp. 2d 1095.

[62] Id. at 1101.

[63] Id. at 1104.

[64] Id. at 1103 (stating that "the Speech or Debate Clause provides immunity to Members of Congress and their aides for personnel actions taken with respect to employees whose duties are directly related to the due functioning of the legislative process"); see also id. at 1104 (stating that "the personnel actions taken by [the Office] against the Plaintiff are afforded Speech or Debate Clause immunity").

[65] Bastien II, 390 F.3d at 1315.

[66] Id. at 1316 (citing Gravel, 408 U.S. at 619-21).

[67] Id. (stating that "[t]o extend protection to informal information gathering ... would be the equivalent of extending Speech or Debate Clause immunity to debates before local radio stations or Rotary Clubs").

[68] Id.

[69] Id. at 1315-16.

[70] Id. at 1319 (stating that "[i]n any event, even under the Browning formulation, Plaintiff here prevails, because her job duties do not satisfy the Gravel standard for legislative act").

[71] An en banc proceeding is one "with all judges present and participating; in full court." BLACK'S LAW DICTIONARY, 546 (7th ed. 1999).

[72] Fields, 459 F.3d at 3.

[73] Id. at 17; see also id. at 17 (Rodgers, J., concurring); id. at 25-26 (Brown, J., concurring); id. at 18 (Tatel, J., concurring).

[74] Id. at 17; see also id. at 17 (Rodgers, J., concurring); id. at 25-26 (Brown, J., concurring); id. at 18 (Tatel, J., concurring).

[75] Fields, 459 F.3d at 14-16.

[76] See Texas Dep't of Cmty. Affairs v. Burdine, 450 U.S. 248, 253-56 (1981); see also McDonnell Douglas Corp. v. Green, 411 U.S. 792 (1973).

[77] Fields, 459 F.3d at 15-16.

[78] Id. at 14 (citing Brewster, 408 U.S. at 508; Brown & Williamson v. Williams, 62 F.3d 408, 415 n. 5 (D.C. Cir. 1995) (stating that "[e]ven when properly subject to suit, members of Congress are privileged against the evidentiary use against them of any legislative act, even if the act is not claimed to be itself illegal, but is offered only to show motive....")); see also Helstoski, 442 U.S. at 487-89; Johnson, 383 U.S. at 169.

[79] Judge Randolph's opinion indicates that an affidavit should be submitted from a person eligible to invoke the Clause and that it should indicate the "legislative activity" or integral part of the legislative process the plaintiffs suit will require inquiry into. See Fields, 459 F.3d at 15-17.

[80] Id. at 17-18.

[81] Id. at 26 (Brown, J., concurring).

[82] Id. at 27 (Brown, J., concurring).

[83] Id.

[84] Id. at 32 (Brown, J., concurring) (stating that "[b]ecause the members are not defendants, the suits do not burden them with defense costs nor place them at any risk of personal liability, and as long as members and their aides are not themselves 'questioned,' an inquiry into legislative acts does not implicate the Speech or Debate Clause." (internal citations omitted)).

[85] Id. (stating that "[w]e need not explore the precise contours of this privilege today; the district court may address these problems as they arise").

[86] See Congressional Accountability Act, P.L. 104-1 § 412, 109 Stat. 3 (1995) (codified at 2 U.S.C. § 1412 (2000)) (stating that "[a]n appeal may be taken directly to the Supreme Court of the United States from any interlocutory or final judgment, decree, or order of a court upon the constitutionality of any provision of this chapter.").

[87] See Office of Senator Dayton v. Hanson, 549 U.S. 1177 (2007).

[88] Dayton v. Hanson, 550 U.S. 511 (2007). Technically, the Court's decision was by a vote of 8-0 with Chief Justice Roberts not participating, as he had been a member of the D.C. Circuit when it rendered its decision in this case.

[89] Congressional Accountability Act, P.L. 104-1 § 412, 109 Stat. 3 (1995) (codified at 2 U.S.C. § 1412 (2000)) (emphasis added).

[90] Dayton, 550 U.S. at 514.

[91] Id. (comparing Fields, 459 F.3d 1 (case below), with Bastien II, 390 F.3d 1301).

[92] Hanson v. Office of Dayton, 535 F. Supp. 2d 25 (D.D.C. 2008).

[93] See, e.g.,Pat Doyle, Questions Over Deal in Suit Against Dayton; Suit Involved Firing of Staffer During US Senate Term, STAR TRIBUNE, Oct. 12, 2010, at 4B.

[94] Fields v. Office of Johnson, 520 F. Supp. 2d 101 (D.D.C. 2007).

[95] Fields v. Office of Johnson, 2008 U.S. App. LEXIS 1107 (D.C. Cir. 2008).

[96] Allegations included wire fraud or conspiracy to commit wire fraud and bribery or conspiracy to bribe a public official and a foreign official. These actions would be in violation of 18 U.S.C. §§ 201, 371, 343, 1346, 1349; 15 U.S.C. § 78dd-1.

[97] Unless otherwise noted, the sources for the factual background herein related are as follows: The Affidavit in Support of Application of Search Warrant, dated May 18, 2006 [hereinafter Affidavit]; the Memorandum in Support of Motion for Return of Property, dated May 24, 2006 on behalf of Representative William J. Jefferson [hereinafter Jefferson Memo]; and the Government's Response to Representative William Jefferson's Motion for Return of Property, dated May 30, 2006 [hereinafter DOJ Response]. The search was authorized by a warrant issued by Chief Judge Thomas Hogan of the United States District Court for the District of Columbia on May 18, 2006.

[98] Jefferson Memo, supra footnote 97, at 3-8; see also DOJ Response, supra footnote 97, at ¶ 4.

[99] It appears that no warrant to search a congressional office had ever been sought or obtained before.

[100] Additional procedures were proposed after Representative Jefferson objected that the filter team might make unilateral determinations about privilege. The additional procedures provided counsel with copies of all material seized from the office and stated that any dispute over privilege would be resolved by the court. See DOJ Response, supra note 48, at 11-12.

[101] Reckless Justice: Did the Saturday Night Raid of Congress Trample the Constitution, Hearing Before the House Comm. on the Judiciary, 109th Cong., 2d Sess. (May 30, 2006) (written testimony of Mr. Bruce Fein at 3-4) available at, http://judiciary.house.gov/OversightTestimony.aspx?ID=637.

[102] The House General Counsel filed as amicus curiae on behalf of the House Bipartisan Leadership Council, in support of Rep. Jefferson's claims.

[103] Jefferson Memo, supra footnote 97 at 13.

[104] Id.

[105] DOJ Response, supra footnote 97, at 14-17 (stating that "the procedures proposed to be used by the Government are plainly sufficient to protect against any permissible intrusion").

[106] Id. at 17-18 (stating that "even if the Speech or Debate Clause were understood to create a criminal discovery privilege, rather than a privilege protecting legislators against being questioned about privileged information or having such information used against them (a point the Government does not concede), it simply does not constitute 'discovery' for a law enforcement agent unconnected with the investigation to make a cursory review of privileged information solely for the purpose of determining whether it is privileged").

[107] Id. at 14. DOJ's assertion with respect to the development and use of House Rule VIII appears to discount the significant historical precedent and evidence that suggests the House of Representatives have nearly always taken a strong position with respect to the release of information in response to requests and subpoenas by the executive branch. Namely, it appears that the House has consistently defended its right to make the first determination with respect to the application of the Speech or Debate privilege. See CRS General Distribution Memorandum, Legal and Constitutional Issues Raised by Executive Branch Searches of Legislative Offices, 13-22, by Morton Rosenberg, Jack H. Maskell, and Todd B. Tatelman (June 13, 2006) (copies available from author on request).

[108] Id. at 23.

[109] Id. at 17 (arguing that "[b]ecause such officials are under affirmative obligations not to disclose the contents of any documents they see (and to attest that they have not done so), there is no prejudice to Rep. Jefferson as a result of the way in which the search was carried out." citing Weatherford v. Bursey, 429 U.S. 545, 556-58 (1977)).

[110] Id. at 21 (arguing that "[i]t has never been suggested that the Constitution is offended merely because members of the prosecution team review legislative materials in the course of making privilege determinations").

[111] In Re: Search of the Rayburn House Office Building Room 2113, Washington, D.C. 20515, No. 06-213, slip op. 1 (D.D.C. July 10, 2006).

[112] Id. at 12.

[113] Id. at 14. The court relied on Fifth Amendment case law for this analysis and concluded that "[j]ust as a search warrant does not trigger the Fifth Amendment's testimonial privilege, neither does a search trigger the Speech or Debate Clause's testimonial privilege. Id. at 15.

[114] Id. at 16.

[115] Id. at 17.

[116] The resolution of Representative Jefferson's appeal appears to have been expedited due to an announcement by the Attorney General that set a July 26, 2006, deadline for investigators to begin reviewing the documents and materials seized from the Representative's House office. See Kenneth P. Doyle, DOJ Complying with Appeals Court Order; Review of Jefferson Search Materials Put Off, BNA MONEY & POLITICS REPORT, 2 (Aug. 1, 2006), available at, http://pubs.bna.com/ip/bna/mpr.nsf/eh/A0B3B3Y4F0.

[117] See United States v. Rayburn House Office Building Room 2113, Washington, D.C. 20515, No. 06-3105 slip op. 1 (D.C. Cir. July 28, 2006). Specifically, the Court of Appeals ordered that the District Court copy all of the paper documents seized by the FBI, as well as provide a list of responsive computer documents to Representative Jefferson for his review. Moreover, the Court of Appeals ordered that Representative Jefferson, within two days of receipt of said documents and records, submit ex parte any claims of privilege under the Speech or Debate Clause. According to the order, the District Court would then conduct an in camera review of the claims and make any and all necessary findings regarding whether the specific documents are legislative in nature and, therefore, privileged. Finally, the Court of Appeals enjoined the DOJ from reviewing any of the documents or materials seized pending further order of the court.

[118] See United States v. Rayburn House Office Building, Room 2113, Washington, D.C. 20515, No. 06-3105, slip op. (D.C. Cir. 2007). Merits briefs were filed by both Representative Jefferson and the DOJ. In addition, amicus curiae (friend of the court) briefs, supporting Representative Jefferson's legal position on the Speech or Debate Clause, were filed by the following individuals: Stanley M. Brand, Christopher Bryant, Steven F. Huefner, Thomas E. Mann, Norman J. Ornstein, Steven R. Ross, Thomas J. Suplak, Charles Tiefer, the Honorable Thomas S. Foley, the Honorable Newt Gingrich, the Honorable Robert H. Michel, the Honorable Abner J. Mikva, Scott Palmer, Elliot Berke, and Reid Stuntz. In support of the DOJ, the Washington Legal Foundation, Judicial Watch, and the Citizens for Responsibility and Ethics in Washington each filed amicus curiae briefs. The House General Counsel, who filed as amicus curiae on behalf of the House Bi-Partisan Leadership Council before the District Court, did not file a brief before the D.C. Circuit.

[119] Id. at 3.

[120] 62 F.3d 408 (D.C. Cir. 1995).

[121] See United States v. Rayburn House Office Building, Room 2113, Washington, D.C. 20515, No. 06-3105, slip op. at 12 (D.C. Cir. 2007) (citing Brown & Williamson, 62 F.3d at 419).

[122] Id. at 13.

[123] Id. at 14.

[124] Id. at 15.

[125] Id. at 16.

[126] Id. at 17 (stating that "[h]ow that accommodation is to be achieved is best determined by the legislative and executive branches in the first instance").

[127] Id. at 17. The court notes, however, that this conclusion is at least in part based on the assertion of the Executive that no agent of the Executive has seen any of the electronic documents or will see them until claims of privilege have been adjudicated. See id. at 17-18.

[128] Id. at 20 (citing Brewster, 408 U.S. at 528).

[129] Id. at 21-22.

[130] Id. at 23 (internal quotations and citations omitted). In light of the fact that Representative Jefferson's indictment was filed in the Eastern District of Virginia, which is a court in the Fourth Circuit, it is unclear exactly what binding effect the D.C. Circuit's holdings and remedies will have on that criminal prosecution. Generally speaking, the decisions of one circuit are not binding on the others.

[131] United States v. Jefferson, No. 09-5130, slip. op. 8 (4th Cir. March 26, 2012); Jerry Markon, Ex-Rep. Jefferson (fl-La.) Gets 13 Years in Freezer Cash Case, WASH. POST, Nov. 14, 2009, available at http://www.washingtonpost.com/ wp-dyn/content/article/2009/11/13/AR2009111301266.html.

[132] Jefferson, slip. op. at 64.

[133] United States v. Renzi, 651 F.3d 1012, 1018 (9th Cir. 2011).

[134] Id. at 1017-18.

[135] Id. at 1017.

[136] Id. at 1018. The hearing Representative Renzi requested was modeled after the type of hearing established in Kastigar v. United States, 406 U.S. 441 (1972), which is used to determine if the government has used any immunized testimony or evidence deriving from immunized testimony to further the prosecution of a person who was granted immunity in exchange for testimony in a separate case. Renzi, 651 F.3d at 1018.

[137] Id. at 1022-23.

[138] Id. at 1021 (citing Brewster, 408 U.S. at 513-14).

[139] Id. at 1022 (citing Helstoski, 442 U.S. at 489-90).

[140] Id. at 1023.

[141] Id. at 1023-24. Representative Renzi failed to convince the appeals court that Brewster did not control application of the Clause in this case because he was charged with extortion rather than bribery. The court cited a Third Circuit case in adopting the conclusion that Brewster applies equally to bribery and extortion charged. Id. at 1024 (citing United States v. McDade, 28 F.3d 283, 296 n. 16 (3rd Circuit 1994).

[142] Renzi, 651 F.3d at 1029 (citing United States v. Swindall, 971 F.2d 1531, 1549 (11th Cir. 1992)).

[143] Id.

[144] Id. at 1032.

[145] Id. at 1034 ("Simply stated, we cannot agree with our esteemed colleagues on the D.C. Circuit. We disagree with both Rayburn's premise and its effect and thus decline to adopt its rationale.").

[146] Id.

[147] Id. at 1036.

[148] Id. at 1036-37. The court also noted that preventing investigations prosecutions for Members who are accused of bribery and similar charges "is unlikely to enhance legislative independence," which is the primary purpose of the Clause. Id. at 1036 (quoting Brewster, 408 U.S. at 524-25).

[149] 442 U.S 477.

[150] Id. at 488 n.7.

[151] Renzi, 651 F.3d at 1037.

[152] Id. at 1037-38.

[153] Id. at 1038.

[154] Id.

[155] Id.

[156] Id. at 1038-39.

[157] Renzi v. United States, 132 S. Ct. 1097 (2012).

INDEX

T

U

V

W

Y